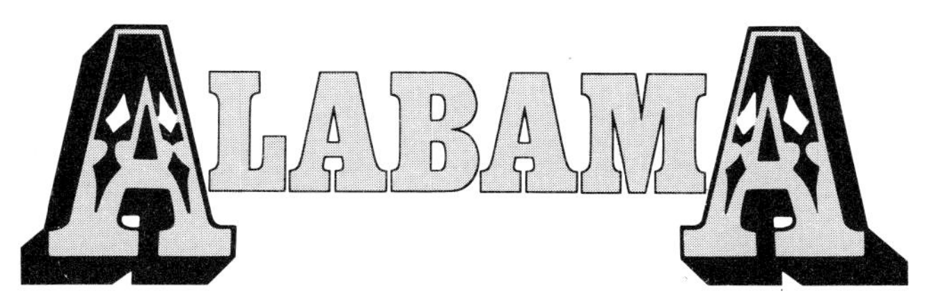
ALABAMA

AF616470

CONTEMPORARY
BOOKS, INC.
CHICAGO

Library of Congress Cataloging in Publication Data

Morris, Edward, 1935–
Alabama.

Includes index.
1. Alabama (Musical group) 2. Country musicians—United States—Biography. I. Title.
ML421.A37M7 1985 784.5'2'00922 [B] 84-29312
ISBN 0-8092-5306-2

For more information about Alabama
write to:
Alabama Band Fan Club
P.O. Box 529
Fort Payne, Alabama 35967
or phone:
(205) 845-1646

Published by Contemporary Books, Inc.
180 North Michigan Avenue, Chicago, Illinois 60601
Manufactured in the United States of America
Library of Congress Catalog Card Number: 84-29312
International Standard Book Number: 0-8092-5306-2

Published simultaneously in Canada by Beaverbooks, Ltd.
195 Allstate Parkway, Valleywood Business Park
Markham, Ontario L3R 4T8 Canada

CONTENTS

**This book is dedicated to
Norma Morris
. . . as is its author**

ACKNOWLEDGMENTS

This book did not begin as a family project, but it soon enough became one. My wife, Norma Morris, a seasoned editor and an occasional photographer, steered me along the twisting paths of photo clearances. And she reminded me, when I most needed it, that in time I could expect a book to coalesce from the papery fragments I despaired over. Erin, my oldest daughter and a publicist for Alabama's record label, was an ever dependable friend and fact-finder. My son Jason suggested and made some useful contacts for me, ran errands, and (once or twice) did my laundry so I could concentrate on these slightly more esoteric laundry lists. Rachel, my youngest daughter, was and is a member of Alabama's fan club, and as such imparted her newsletters and insights to me. Moreover, she let me know how proud she was that after all these years I was finally writing about something important.

Many of my fellow journalists shared their notes and recollections of Alabama with me, including Kip Kirby (who put me onto the book in the first place), Pat Harris, Vernell Hackett, Barry Bronson, and Neil Pond. Others whose tips and interviews were essential are Scott Tutt, Willie Rainsford, Ed Turbeville, Betty Cook, Elaine Herndon, Joe Taylor, Ethel Reaves, Ronnie Pugh, Roger McDowell, Dick Beacham, and Rita Adrian.

I want to give a most heartfelt tribute to my mother, Mary Morris; she has faithfully supported me in whatever the lunacy I might be engaged, and "toughed it" through a series of illnesses without my company while I was beating distant bushes for the material you have here.

Edward Morris
Nashville
November 1984

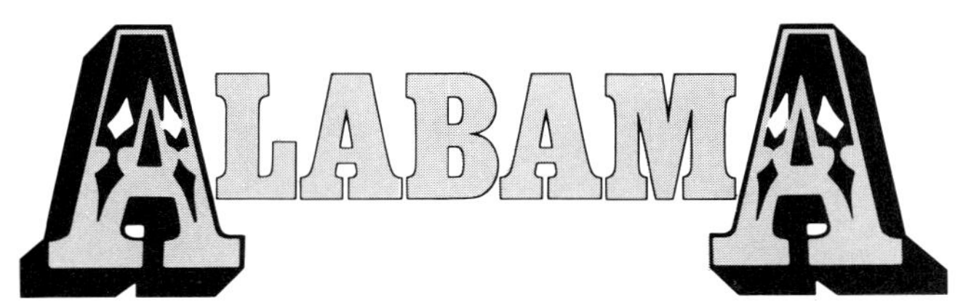
ALABAMA

Jim Rawlings

Jim Rawlings

Jim Rawlings

Jim Rawlings

CHAPTER 1

ALABAMA: ONE BY ONE

After all the years of working and waiting for recognition, Alabama has evolved into something that is more to its members than merely a mechanism for making money and music. The group's success is a heartfelt memorial to Randy Owen's father, Gladstone, who knew all along that his boy and his buddies had the talent to make a name for themselves. Alabama has become a fortress against the world's slights and ills and a rallying cry of regional pride. "My Home's in Alabama" is, as it turns out, less the statement of a geographic place than the assertion of a psychological one.

It is almost as if the concept of Alabama overtook four boys who were neither much better nor much worse than other boys their age and turned them collectively into men of greater stature than any of them could have achieved alone. Because most people came to know Alabama as the unit they worked so hard to polish and strengthen, focusing on the remarkable differences in the four individual personalities is difficult.

Paul Natkin/Photo Reserve

RANDY OWEN

Those eyes.

When the sound of his voice and the details of his conversation fade, everyone is left with the vivid memory of Randy Owen's dark, liquid eyes. From under the ledge of black bangs and the ruler-straight brows, those eyes scroll across the world in front of them with benevolent curiosity, melting the skepticism and quickening the hearts of those who look back at him with their dull, ordinary eyes, making people feel that until Owen gazed at them they had enjoyed from other eyes only glances.

At a safe distance back from those riveting eyes, you can glimpse the college-jock, young-puppy playfulness of Owen, especially when he is bounding and bouncing onto the stage to accept this or that prize for yet another Alabama milestone. Standing off to the side in the jersey and jeans he so favors, Owen could pass for a high school coach, still reminiscing about his own hot days at the line of scrimmage, still almost in good shape, save for a soft spot here or a thick one there.

But where Owen transcends all the types he reminds you of is at the microphone when he is telling you—just you, and nobody else in that beseeching crowd—about the heartaches that brought him to you at this moment, or warning you how your indifference can make your lady down on love. In these earnest exchanges of confidence, he is like nobody else. And the eyes confirm it anew.

Possessing one of the most intimate voices in country music, Owen's sound is a cross between Merle Haggard's hard-edged attack on lyrics and Hoyt Axton's almost oratorical resonance. He can croon and caress a line down to a clear, urgent whisper or boom out a manifesto—like "My Home's in Alabama"—as if he's delivering a sermon to the sinners in the back row.

Many observers think Alabama begins and ends with Randy Owen, in spite of the fact that Jeff Cook is the senior member of the group and its best picker. Of the four, Randy seems to be the one who could most easily switch to a solo career. But this is not a prospect he's considered—at least not publicly.

Alabama's lead singer, Randy Owen.

Photo courtesy of Jacksonville State University

In interviews, Owen invariably emerges as the most thoughtful of the four—the one who has put it all into perspective and digested it to the point that even a novice reporter can go away from the interview thinking that he or she has been able to grasp the essence of Alabama.

Owen's sense of restraint and diplomacy also balance the whimsy—and occasional surliness—of Cook and drummer Mark Herndon. When veteran country music writer Bob Allen was ready to unplug his tape recorder and call it quits because Cook and Herndon took him to task for asking a question about the band's legal problems, Owen stepped in gracefully to explain the frustration that the other two could only reflect. Teddy Gentry, who talks well about the nuts and bolts of the business and who has been called upon more than once to testify in court about Alabama's finances, also seems to defer to Owen in group interviews, sensing perhaps that Owen's even

Randy Owens decorates the tree.

temper and ease with words always make for the safest bet.

His love of words and facility in using them have made Owen the most productive songwriter in the group—although all the others are represented in the albums. In Alabama's first five albums for RCA Records—from *My Home's in Alabama* through *Roll On*—Owen's name is on 15 of the 50 songs, either as sole writer or cowriter. He takes total credit for "Tennessee River," "Feels So Right," "Mountain Music," "Lady Down on Love," "Carolina Mountain Dewe," and "Food on the Table." And he is a contributor to "My Home's in Alabama," "Hanging Up My Travelin' Shoes," "Get It While It's Hot," "Fantasy," "I'm Stoned," "You Turn Me On," "Very Special Love," "I'm Not That Way Anymore" (Herndon's only inclusion, to date), and "The Boy."

Early Years

Growing up poor near Adamsburg, Alabama, in an area where being poor brought you neither shame nor distinction, Owen got his first taste of music listening to his father and mother sing. The family had no radio until Randy was 12 or so, but he recalls hearing gospel records of the Louvin Brothers. Music was also a mainstay of the services at the Holiness Church Randy and his cousin Teddy attended. In time, the two would get their first glimpse of stage life by playing and singing at the church.

When radio finally did come to the Owen household, an eager and attentive Randy memorized the songs he heard and studied the harmonies as if he were doing homework—only with infinitely more delight and a far greater sense of discovery. The radio arrived in time for Randy to monitor the best acts Britain had to send, the Beatles among them. As he told reporter Jeff Nesin, "Late at night I used to listen to a station out of Cleveland, Ohio, and they had a British Countdown show—that's when the Beatles were coming out. Boy, I really enjoyed that. It was a big thing for me."

Randy came of age in the 1960s—that fabled period that gave us the "generation gap." It was not a gap that Owen fell into. His parents—and particularly his father, with his examples of hard work and strong principles—endowed him with the stamina and direction he needed to endure all the heartbreaks and discouragements he would encounter. While other kids in more affluent surroundings were concluding that their parents were pathetically beyond redemption, Owen was still learning from his.

Paul Natkin/Photo Reserve

In a conversation with writer Pat Harris, Owen recalled what his father had done for him and how much he still missed him: "I'm the only son in my family and was so close to my dad. He worked so hard. It was really hard. He had seen me struggle along. People made fun of me about making a living playing music—his only son doing that. But he supported me."

Gladstone Owen's death came at the worst, most ironic of times, Randy explained: "He died two weeks before we signed with RCA. . . . So he didn't live long enough to see that. But once he picked me up at the airport. I told him, 'Daddy, I think it's finally going to happen for us.' And he believed me. And as it turned out, I was right."

The relationship between Randy and his father probably was unusual because most fathers in those days supposedly didn't show feelings or communicate with their children. And accordingly most children were rebellious.

Critics may note that Owen's "Food on the Table" is similar in mood and detail to Loretta Lynn's "Coal Miner's Daughter." Indeed, both writers seem to have drawn a profound sense of strength and self-identity from the examples their fathers set.

The result of this closeness to his own father has made him more aware of his importance to his own children. Owen told Harris: "I talk to my kids. . . . When I'm home, I never go anywhere without my kids. Every minute I lose with them is a minute I've lost forever. I don't want my son to reach the age of seven or eight hardly knowing me. I don't want him to not want to go with me. They can't stand it when I leave home. Sad. I'm not happy about it, either, but at least it shows how much we love one another."

Because he had dropped out of high school for a time, Owen didn't graduate until 1969, the same year he and Teddy and Jeff first assembled as a musical group, Young Country. That fall, Owen enrolled in Northeast State Junior College, near Rainsville, only a short distance from his home. He was able to keep a workable balance between his academic and musical existence—even merging the two by earning tuition by finally playing for money instead of for free. One long-time source of income was the Bigham Barn Dance across the nearby Georgia state line in Summerville. It was a job he would later memorialize through a couple of lines in "My Home's in Alabama."

College Years

At Jacksonville State University, about 60 miles southwest of Fort Payne, Owen's love for language and literature started to mature. By the time he transferred there from Northeast State in the early '70s, he had already decided on a musical career. Still, he reasoned, it wouldn't hurt to have a degree to fall back on. Besides, the Asian conflict had made the campus one of the two most exciting places to inhabit, the other being Vietnam.

At Jacksonville State, Owen fell under the influence of Professor Ethel Reaves. Owen never enrolled in her classes, but as his academic adviser, Reaves steered him

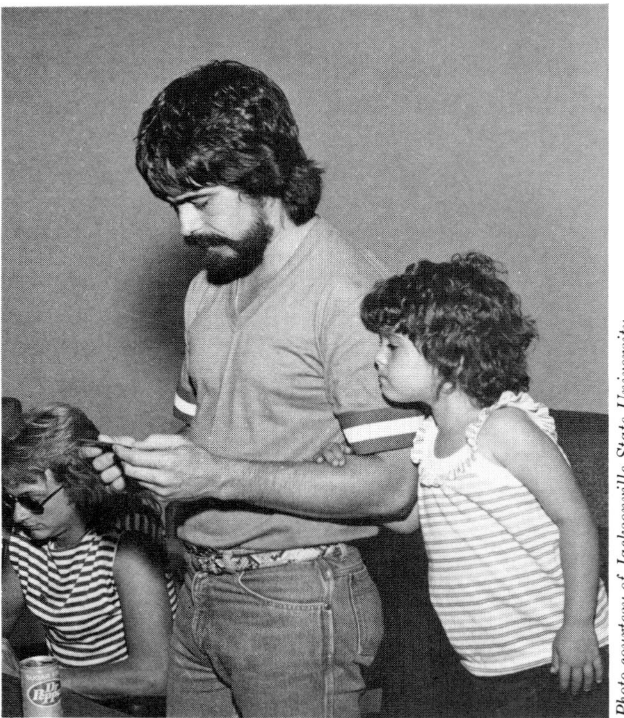

Photo courtesy of Jacksonville State University

An inquisitive Alison Owen checks to see what Daddy Randy is holding, while Alabama's drummmer, Mark Herndon, left, awaits the start of a press conference at Randy's college.

into English and helped him sift out his thoughts and aspirations.

"I first saw him," Reaves related, "when he came into my office and said, 'I want you to help me find a program [in which] I won't have to have a major or minor.' I had never heard such a request, so I asked him, 'Well, what do you plan to do?' He said, 'I want to make music. That's all I care about. That's my life.' "

A very puzzled Professor Reaves continued to query the intense young man: "After he convinced me that that was what he wanted to do, I said, 'Why don't you go ahead and get on with your music now? I wouldn't stay here if it didn't mean anything.' He said, 'I've always said I would get a college degree—I wouldn't think of not having one. But music is my life, and that's what I intend to pursue.' So being in English myself, I majored him in English."

The prof and the poor boy got along well

Lisa Brown, of the Jacksonville State University Alumni Association, presents a lifetime alumni membership card to Randy Owen.

from the start. "He was just easy to talk with," Reaves remembered. "He didn't have a beard then. And I remember thinking he was such a good-looking little old boy. He had the prettiest eyes."

Returning to Jacksonville State in 1982 with Alabama to play a concert there and to accept a lifetime membership in the alumni association, Owen did some recalling of his own on his life as a student/musician: "I was playing back then, but nobody cared." According to Owen, he wrote songs in the library while he was supposed to be studying. He wrote a lot of songs there that haven't been recorded. But there was one that made it to vinyl.

Reaves said Owen brought her a song once that he "was playing . . . in these smoky bars, [and] he thought it would go somewhere. So I said, 'Sing it.' He said, 'I can't sing without my guitar.' I said, 'Why don't you just tell me the words and let me see what I think about it.' He talked it off, and I thought it was the corniest song I'd ever heard. You know what it was? 'Feels So Right.' Shows you what I knew about it.

"I was impressed with him because he was so determined," Reaves continued. "I remember one day he sat in the office a long time, and I was trying to tell him what to do. I said, 'Listen, don't sing those loud songs where you yell in them. Sing like Engelbert Humperdinck.' He said, 'I don't like Engelbert Humperdinck.' Well, he came back down here one day for a concert. He was talking on the radio about his old teachers he remembered. I was here [at home] peeling potatoes, and I heard him say, 'Well, I remember Mrs. Reaves.' I was excited he remembered me. . . . I couldn't go to the concert, but my husband went backstage to see Randy. And the first thing Randy asked

Jim Rawlings

Randy Owen being amused.

was 'Does she still collect Engelbert Humperdinck records?' And my husband said, 'No—she collects yours.' "

Through the many conversations Reaves had with her talented advisee, one factor remained constant: "Every time we ever talked it was always about his music. . . . I don't think I ever saw a student who was as determined as he was. He had that very determined look."

Many years after her sessions with Owen had ended and he was reaping the victories of his determination, Mrs. Reaves was in England, studying Shakespeare, and a young girl happened to notice her Southern accent. "She asked me if I lived near Fort Payne, Alabama, and I told her the whole story. So this young girl ran over to where some of her friends were standing and brought them back to me, squealing, 'She knows Randy Owen!' "

In a characteristic burst of generosity, Owen recently established a $1,000-a-year scholarship at Jacksonville State for English majors who keep up at least a C-plus average. The gift should help some young determined dreamer who might otherwise be overlooked in the academic merry-go-round. "Don't be afraid to chase dreams," Owen told the students at JSU. To the teachers, he counseled, "Encourage the student who is a little different."

Social Consciousness

By the time Owen graduated from college in 1973 (with a B average), campuses across the country were cooling down, just as the Vietnam war was winding down. About that time, the dominant campus concern switched from wanting to change the world to wanting to find a good job. Owen found a job with Cook, Gentry, and Bennett Vartanian at the Bowery in Myrtle Beach—a job he would stick with through a roller coaster of uncertainties for the next seven years.

But his father's values, the ragtag ends of the campus ferment of the '60s, and his own developing outlook on the world all implanted a social and political consciousness in Owen that still serves him today. He lobbied to get "Changes Comin' On"—a respectful, if moderate, appraisal of '60s concerns—on Alabama's *Mountain Music* album, partly for its message and partly for its crossover potential.

Owen has spoken out for better treatment of Vietnam veterans, reasoning this way: "People are gonna start talking more about Vietnam. A lot of people got killed unnecessarily, and we'll never be able to pay back those vets, because they fought without any moral support, practically none."

In this same interview with reporter Lane Lambert, Owen made it clear that he was still learning about his place in the social process: "When we went to Detroit to do a concert, this older man came up and said, 'I can't believe you boys claim to love America, especially being from the South, and you're driving a Mercedes truck.' He was talking about one of the equipment trucks. There was something about the way he said that—there was a lot of hurt in his voice. That really struck me. That's why as long as I live there'll never be a dollar of my money spent for a foreign car. That's the least I can do. Those people support us." Hearing that a benefit auction for laid-off steelworkers in Pennsylvania was in need of items, Alabama promptly dispatched a shipment—"Not as a political thing," Owen explained, "just for the people."

When reporter Michelle Broussard asked the members of Alabama what each would like for Christmas, Owen responded with a veritable platform of social wishes: "I'd like all the problems in South America to be settled. I'd like to see them solved so we won't have to get so involved. And I would like to see changes made as far as the way old people are treated in the nursing homes. I'd like to see more care given to the elderly, to people who have worked hard all their lives. They should be able to live in dignity in their retirement years, rather than having to scratch and just get by. It's something that's real important to me."

Ever the realist, Owen is quite willing to discuss the chilling notion that some day Alabama may lose its great popularity. It's a prospect he has come to terms with. As he told writer Lane Lambert: ". . . I don't expect in my heart that all this is gonna last forever. It can't. History isn't going to change for us. There will come a time when we won't be as popular. People outgrow you."

To writer Jack Hurst, Owen wrapped it all up: "If anything ever happened to Alabama, I could go back and work side by side with those people who've got two or three kids, get up at six every morning, and manage to eke out enough money to come out to one of our shows or buy one of our records. We've been blessed to the extent that that's something I'd probably never have to do, but I don't think I'm too good to do it."

Larry Dixon

JEFF COOK

Party boy. Equipment freak. Musical maniac. Wisecracker. Flirt. Diet disaster.

Don't bother choosing one or two of the above. In Jeff Cook, you get them all. Cook is the one buzzing fly in Alabama's rags-to-riches ointment. Teddy and Randy were raised poor and country, but Jeff was strictly middle-class and small-town, a veritable aristocrat by comparison. But when it comes to his musical background, Cook's credentials are just as down-and-dirty as anybody else's. He was out there on the road and in the studio paying dues while Randy and Teddy were still picking beans and wondering just what the hell it would take to get off the farm.

Talented Youth

Jeff's mother, Betty, recalled what it was like, trying to raise her young musical dynamo: "I used to rock him to sleep and play 'Good Night Irene.' I had one of those [phonographs] you just lifted the needle over on—it wasn't automatic—and I'd sit there and play that thing a dozen times, rocking him to sleep." All that musical exposure began to pay off as Cook grew up. "When Jeff was six years old, he got on the stage at Williams Avenue School and sang 'You Ain't Nothin' but a Hound Dog.' I started giving him piano lessons when he was small, but his music teacher told me, 'There's no need of that kid taking music—he's got it in his bones.' "

Mrs. Cook related that one day she had the radio on in the living room where the piano was. Jeff (who was still quite young) came in, sat down at the piano, and started playing the song that was on the radio. "I couldn't believe my ears." Before the age at which most boys are coming to terms with a razor, Jeff had already formed such hometown groups as the Viscounts and J.C. and The Chosen Few—an especially daring name for a Bible-belt band. Still in his early

Melodie Gimple

Jeff Cook dons a winged hat to keep the show from getting too serious.

teens, the tireless young picker was playing bass guitar with the Howell Family gospel group and even venturing into Birmingham to cut records with them.

Then there was his eight-year (on-and-off) career as a disc jockey: "I started three days after I was 14." Cook remembers, "working the night shift at WFPA in Fort Payne. I worked at both stations in Fort Payne, one in Rainsville [Alabama], and at WYAK in Myrtle Beach [South Carolina] while Wildcountry was performing at the Bowery."

Cook continued to pick and sing his way through his later teens. With cousins Randy and Teddy, Jeff won a talent contest at a local high school, which earned them all a trip to the Grand Ole Opry. The high point of that pilgrimage, as one of them later recalled, was meeting the legendary bluegrass stylist, Lester Flatt.

Back in those days, according to Mrs. Cook, the boys traveled to their gigs in a

Pat Rawlings

A Christmassy Jeff Cook.

manner conspicuously more modest than the one they have since embraced: "Before any of them could drive, my husband [James] took the boys in a station wagon to all those little school dances. He'd sit out in the car and wait on them until midnight."

Jeff graduated from high school in 1967—two years before he and his country cousins would start the casual jam session that would one day lead to the sale of more than 14 million record albums. If there was a corresponding passion to the one he held for music, it was the study of electronics. Following high school, Cook enrolled at Alabama Technical College in Gadsden; and in 1970, earned his diploma in electronics.

After graduating, Cook took a job with Western Electric in Huntsville, later transferring to a post in Anniston. His apartment in nearby Bynum became yet another hub of music—just as his parent's house had been—when Randy (who was in college) and Teddy (who was laying carpet) moved in with him. In early 1972, Jeff, Teddy, Randy, and Bennett Vartanian officially launched Wildcountry, and a year later they all decided to chuck their day jobs and become full-time performers at the Bowery.

Picking and Singing

Jeff's picking and range of vocal harmonizing have always been the musical bedrock of Alabama (no matter what the group might have been called at the time). He is proficient on lead and rhythm guitar, piano, organ, fiddle, and bass—at last count. And there is some slight hint that he might be able to play the accordion—if he ever felt vicious enough to do so. Recollecting to Michelle Broussard about one of his childhood Christmas presents, he quipped: "I remember one year when I got a toy accordion. You know what they say about accordions? 'If you own one, have the good taste not to play it!' So I'd hide it under my bed."

On stage, the portly Cook is a blur of activity, switching from this instrument to that in midsong, consistently lending his voice to that sweet Alabama blend, reeling off vocal impressions, and grinning out at the audience with that fine set of teeth prosperity has brought him. Once asked by a fan if he minded having his picture taken so often, Cook candidly responded, "No. I spent $5,000 on these teeth so I could smile."

A tad on the heavy side at the time Alabama first came to national prominence, Cook has since ballooned to Falstaffian proportions. In the early Bowery days, those who knew him estimate that he weighed no more than 120 pounds, soaked with sweat. In fact, the owner of Duffy's Tavern, next door to the Bowery, still has on his wall a picture of the group, showing a quite recognizable Owen and Gentry but a strangely miniaturized lead guitarist.

Although the members of Alabama play very little on their albums—electing instead to trust the speed and artistic instincts of Nashville's top studio musicians—Cook is more likely than any of the others to con-

Paul Natkin/Photo Reserve

tribute instrumentals to the records. He is a good enough picker to have been invited to appear on non-Alabama projects. So far, he has declined.

As he told Jack Hurst, "I had a chance to do an instrumental album with James Burton [the guitarist who has worked with Elvis Presley, Merle Haggard, and many other stars], and we could still do that any time. It wouldn't really be fair, though. I'd be upset if Randy or Teddy went and cut a thing on their own—singing, I mean; if they wanted to go play on something, I wouldn't be bothered too much. But I don't think our recording separately [as singers] will happen until the dissolving of the group Alabama and maybe not even then. We've got a good formula that's working. Why mess with it?"

As a songwriter, Cook has been fairly active. He is writer or cowriter of eight of the 50 songs on Alabama's first five RCA albums: "See the Embers, Feel the Flame," "Lovin' You Is Killin' Me," "Fantasy," "Lovin' Man," "Some Other Place, Some Other Time," "Very Special Love," "Keep on Dreamin'," and "Get It While It's Hot."

Wisecracks and Dreams

In 1982, Cook realized a long-time dream

Jeff Cook's recording studio (entrance, above) is housed in this barn-shaped structure (below) on Lookout Mountain.

Edward Morris

Paul Natkin/Photo Reserve

when he opened the doors to his 24-track Cook Sound Studios up on narrow, winding Scenic Road on Lookout Mountain. Fort Payne not being a recording center, the studios have seen a minimum of profitable activity, although some tracks for the *Roll On* album were cut there

No doubt remembering his own radio days, Cook has applied to the Federal Communications Commission for a license to open a 10,000-watt AM station near Fort Payne. He told one interviewer that if he got his own radio station going he would program everything he listened to on pop radio in the '60s: the Beatles, a little bit of Motown, and Paul Revere and the Raiders.

Writers who interview Alabama in a group can bet that before the interview is over, Cook will be making his wisecracks and one-liners—unless he's hungry or eager to get out and jam with some local bar band.

Music City News editor Barry Bronson went on the road with Alabama once to see what the group dynamics were like. On this particular run, the group played a packed concert at Eastern Illinois University on a hot, muggy evening. Following the show, the weary lads signed autographs for nearly an hour and a half, and finally got back to their motel rooms well past one in the morning. For one of the boys, Bronson reports, the day was still young: "Cook ducks into the Charleston Inn lounge to pick a few songs with the house band. He just got through an exhausting show and now he's playing again in a dark, smoky lounge."

Larry Dixon

TEDDY GENTRY

On a late winter morning in 1983, one-time poor boy Teddy Gentry strolled into a Senatobia, Mississippi, auction barn to survey the polled Hereford cattle on sale there. When he left a few hours later with his friend and cousin, Randy Owen, the boy whose family had been too poor to afford even an *outdoor* toilet when he was growing up had spent $22,825 for eleven more cows and three more calves he didn't need. Gentry had made that headiest of odysseys for a country boy: from dirt farmer to gentleman farmer.

Teddy Gentry grew up an only child—unless, of course, you want to count the constant companionship of second cousin Randy Owen. The two were Huck-and-Tom buddies well before they realized they had a gift of making fine music together. Randy was poor enough, but Teddy was even poorer. Since slim living was pretty well par for the neighborhood, Teddy says he was never really aware of how little his family—headed by his mother and grandfather—really had.

The man who could drop more than $20,000 in a single day of cattle-buying can still conjure up the image of a little boy and his grandfather picking tomatoes for two weeks to earn enough money to buy a second-hand television set. He was able, in the years to come, to joke with Loretta Lynn about how relatively lavish her upbringing had been. After all, he told her, she at least had an outhouse—all he'd had was the outdoors and a talent for remembering where he'd stopped the night before.

Singing in Church and Contests

Before Teddy was born, his mother and father got a divorce; his mom then moved back in with her father on the skimpy 80-acre farm on Lookout Mountain. Teddy was 17 when he first met his father.

Like Randy, who preferred the company

Jim Rawlings

Teddy Gentry ponders an interviewer's question.

of his slightly younger cousin to that of his two sisters, Teddy got his musical start in church—at first watching others perform, later playing the guitar and singing himself. He says he learned the rudiments of his chording and picking style by watching church members (such as Randy's father) playing and then running home to duplicate as much as he could remember.

Teddy would not meet his fourth cousin, Jeff, until he went to high school, by which time many of his musical tastes and traits had been formed; but like Jeff Cook, Teddy did his share of experimenting with local bands.

Roger McDowell, who now runs a pawn shop in Fort Payne, was in one of those early bands with Teddy. He played the Bowery at Myrtle Beach in '67. "This was a long time before their band [Jeff, Teddy, and Randy's] was ever formed. I was with a group called the Malibu's—me and Bennett Vartanian and a couple of others played in the Bowery

Jim Rawlings

Teddy Gentry posing for a Christmas layout.

there for about five or six years. When Bennett came home from the army, me and him and Teddy got together and formed a group called the Sand Mountain Chickenpluckers. I played lead, Teddy played bass, and Bennett played drums."

The Chickenpluckers were not immediately set upon by music critics and cultural historians, but they did manage to find themselves employment. They got a job in a little supper club in Chattanooga, playing three nights a week. They got $40 a week—plus, McDowell notes, ". . . well, the bottom line was our drinks and all the catfish we could eat. We did that for a long time.

"And then one night down here in Fort Payne, me and Teddy came in, and they were having a battle of the bands. We didn't go there to get in the battle, but I had my guitar in my car. Teddy didn't have his bass, but we decided we were gonna get in the battle. Well, we didn't have a drummer—Bennett wasn't there that night—so Teddy asked this Baker guy he knew if he would play the drums. We went in and asked the people if we could enter the contest, and they said yes. We'd never played drums with this guy. Teddy had to borrow another guy's bass, and I used another guy's amp. But we got up there and ad-libbed as the Sand Mountain Chickenpluckers and won the first-prize trophy. It came out in the paper, you know. Teddy or the Baker boy still has the trophy."

McDowell, who still records on occasion, was deeply involved in that wide and varied pool of Fort Payne musical talent out of which Alabama ultimately emerged: "I worked with Jeff down here at the radio station—WFPA. Me and him were disc jockeys. Before this band that me and Teddy and Bennett had, we also worked at the station out on Sand Mountain. Jeff's real good with electronics. He's a whiz at anything like that. Jerry Lee Lewis came to town one time and did a show here. That was probably back in '66, and Jeff was working at the radio station. Jeff got Jerry Lee to come over to his house, and they cut some tapes."

After high school, Gentry spent a lot of his time with Jeff and Randy, polishing his harmonies and his instrumental licks, playing the now-and-then paying gig that cropped up and otherwise trying to bring professional class to the group that came together in 1972 as Wildcountry.

On stage these days, Gentry projects neither the respectable buffoonery of Jeff Cook nor the smoldering sensuality of Randy Owen. But his is a presence to be

Paul Natkin/Photo Reserve

reckoned with, and his skills as a bassist and harmonica player are instantly evident. Tall, lanky, and almost imperious in his stance, Gentry has eyes that pierce like Owen's but which do not radiate the warmth.

He takes his bass playing most seriously, demanding that it serve the individual song and not a particular type of music. As he told writer Jeff Nesin: "I just don't try to play country bass. I try to play whatever will enhance the song, whatever feels right. For me, an all-around band—and that's the Beatles, Creedence [Clearwater Revival], the Eagles—is a band that's capable of writing their own stuff, playing their own stuff, and singing their own stuff live on stage and still have the harmony there."

As to the effect the band strives for on stage, Gentry added: "We try to be a visual act . . . actually we try to use all the senses, satisfying their ears, their eyes, and their hearts. If we've covered all those areas, then we've done a good show and entertained the people."

When it comes to caring about people, Gentry and Owen run about neck-and-neck; especially when the people are in their own

Paul Natkin/Photo Reserve

families. Just as Owen reveres the memory of his father and grieves he could not have done more for him, Gentry praises his grandfather as "a remarkable man." After Alabama hit it big, one of the first things Gentry did was buy his grandfather's farm from him—for cash—and saw to it that there was enough cash involved so that his grandfather could live off the interest alone. Then he built his mother the brick home she had always wanted. One in which, he wryly noted, there was indoor plumbing.

The same circumstances that gave Gentry the luxury to take care of his mother and grandfather keep him away from his own two kids far more than he's comfortable with, but he tries to impart a sense of normalcy to the family scene by treating his time on the road as just a case of "Daddy going off to work."

In his songwriting, he has been successful in incorporating warm family images into commercial frameworks, particularly in his touchingly tender birthday/growing up ballad, "Never Be One," on the *Mountain Music* album, and his cowriting effort on "The Boy," from the *Roll On* LP.

Gentry's mark is on 12 of the 50 songs on Alabama's first five RCA LPs. Of these, he wrote only two by himself: "Never Be One" and "Ride the Train." The remaining cowritten output includes "My Home's in Alabama," "Hanging Up My Travelin' Shoes," "Why Lady Why," "Get It While It's Hot," "Fantasy," "I'm Stoned," "You Turn Me On," "Very Special Love," "I'm Not That Way Anymore," and "The Boy."

The domestic side of Gentry and his often severe demeanor only partially conceal a fine sense of humor and a quick wit—virtues that can spring to the surface and burst into clowning on stage or tripping up a reporter asking a question that's over-asked or predictable. He assured one such reporter that it was his Christmas tradition to "go into the woods and antique the trees."

On the day he bought his expensive and superfluous cattle in Mississippi, another buyer recognized Gentry and handed him a program to autograph. To alleviate his own nervousness, the man said, "I'll bet you get tired of all this." To which a thoughtful Teddy responded: "No, sir. I don't. I used to lay carpet for a living. I prefer this."

Vernell Hackett

MARK HERNDON

Somewhere along the relative-rich corridor that stretches from Massachusetts to South Carolina, blond beauty Mark Herndon may well have a cousin or two scratching about. But Jeff Cook, Randy Owen, and Teddy Gentry are not among them. Herndon is Alabama's Cinderella. He lucked out—but he ain't one of the family.

Although Herndon is an artistic part of Alabama, he is not a legal part as are the others. He is a salaried employee. This fact isn't to suggest that Herndon is being mistreated like Cinderella. His is just the natural fate of the latecomer. While the other three were grinding out a lumpy existence at the Bowery, a considerably younger Herndon was finishing up high school at Camden Military Academy (in South Carolina) and subsequently taking an exploratory dip in the fountains of higher education at Francis Marion College in Florence, South Carolina.

Born in Springfield, Massachusetts, in 1955, Mark Joel Herndon was destined to enjoy—or suffer—the gypsy life of a military kid. His father was a Marine pilot whose duties took the family from pillar to post. Besides Springfield and Camden and Florence, Mark lived in Cherry Point, North Carolina, and spent a year in Montgomery, Alabama, while his father was in war college there.

As an only child on the move, Herndon developed the shyness and sensitivity of a loner. Growing up, he liked studying and drawing airplanes—and he liked to write, especially when his teachers would let him make up stories. He still fondly recalls his third grade teacher who would cut out magazine pictures for him to develop stories about.

Music, though, was not one of his early consolations or enthusiasms. How did he get into music when he was a little boy? "He didn't," said his mother, Elaine, "except by taking piano lessons. I had a very strong classical background, and so did my mother. We urged and urged and urged Mark, but he would have none of it. I think you could safely say that as far as Mark's drumming goes, he was a very late bloomer." Herndon didn't even think much about becoming a drummer until he was in high school.

Pat Rawlings

Mark Herndon as elf.

By the time he got to Francis Marion College, though, he was ready to bloom. Having no drum set to practice on, he rigged one up in his dorm room, using such throwaways as pillows for drums, a bent coat hanger with a Ping-Pong ball on it for a foot pedal, and slabs of styrofoam packing materials for cymbals.

Of course, he visited every club in the area to see real drummers in action and to study their methods. After he had saved enough money to buy a drum set, he moved to an apartment where he could, and did, jam in earnest. The more he got into drums, the less he got out of school. And in 1976, three years before his wandering ship

Photo courtesy of Ed Turbeville

In the year before he joined Alabama, Mark Herndon (second from right) was the drummer for the Ed Turbeville Orchestra, working out of Florence, SC. That's Turbeville at the microphone.

would dock in Alabama, Herndon dropped out of college.

Herndon's first band job lasted about a year but did nothing to educate him in the ways of being a professional musician. That lofty task was left to bandleader Ed Turbeville.

"Ed was the first mentor I had," Herndon told Rick Mattingly in a revealing *Modern Drummer* article. "He was the first guy I worked for. He taught me a lot about discipline. When I came to him, it was like a drum solo the whole time I was playing. I was more interested in my own chops than in playing for the band. He settled me down and started me thinking 'band.' "

Herndon's mentor, who now heads the Ed Turbeville Super Band in Florence, recalled his time with the young star: "I imagine he played [for me] close to a year. At that time, Mark was the youngest member. I was in the process of hunting a drummer. You know how this business is—you start calling, and I got his name. And when I called him, he just seemed so eager. I tried him out, and I could tell he had a lot of basic ability. But he was pretty rough cut at that time. He had had very, very little experience—almost none. But he seemed so anxious."

The band Herndon had joined tried mightily to be all things to all audiences, according to Turbeville: "We were doing a lot of commercial things—a pretty wide variety of things. We'd do society work—country club work—where we'd play a lot of big band tunes and then turn around and play at a country-and-western-type place. We never did any hardcore country. What we did was a lot of uptown country—Kenny Rogers, Willie Nelson, stuff that had crossed over."

Turbeville's limitation on country music was apparently fine with Herndon, who told a writer for *Country Rhythms* that "I didn't even know who Mel Tillis was when I joined

Mark announces country music nominees for the Grammys at a Nashville press conference.

[Alabama]. I knew nothing. I'd heard of Loretta Lynn and some of the big-time stars. I knew who Roy Clark was, I guess, but I'd never heard of anyone else, really. I'd never paid attention to that kind of music coming up. I was always into *rock*."

Mark's mother was working the registration desk at the Thunderbird Motor Inn in Florence when a less-than-triumphant Alabama rolled in to do a week's engagement in the lounge there. Hearing that the band's drummer had given notice he would be quitting, Mrs. Herndon divulged that she knew a young drummer who might be interested in auditioning for the impending vacancy. She was cool enough to withhold the information that the young applicant was her son. But by the time she had summoned Mark to rush in with his plea for employment, the motel manager had fired Alabama—as the story goes—for failing to play enough disco. When the band called

Mark Herndon signs souvenirs at the annual fan fair in Nashville. *Music City News photo by Neil Pond*

Mark some months later, he was still laboring under the benevolent baton of Ed Turbeville.

"I'll tell you the truth," Turbeville confessed later. "He almost passed up the chance to play with Alabama because he wanted to give me adequate notice. Mark and I had a talk, and I said, 'Well, I don't want you to miss anything, but I need time to get somebody else.' I remember Mark's reply was very unusual for any young man. He said, 'I think too much of you and the band. I'm going on and play out my notice, and if they want me under those conditions, fine, and if they don't, the hell with it.' "

While such an outlook seems professionally suicidal from the vantage point of today, it wasn't in early '79. Turbeville scoffs at the notion that everyone was just waiting then for Alabama to break. "A lot of people around here say, 'I knew they were going to make it.' Hell, nobody knew it. The group was good—there's no getting around that. But they were just like a lot of groups. They happened to be in the right place at the right time. I'm not trying to say they didn't have the caliber. I don't mean that at all. But there are a lot of good groups around that never get the chance to be in the right place. So I had mixed emotions about Mark going with the group. I figured they'd been there [at the Bowery] seven or eight years—and they were still there."

In March, 1979, Mark drove to Myrtle Beach to try out for the band, making a point to arrive several minutes before he was due. He wanted to impress his prospective employers with his punctuality, a quality both his parents and Ed Turbeville had placed great weight on. His skill, Alabama's desperation, or, more likely, a confluence of the two carried the day; Mark officially went to work for the group on April 1.

To this day, Herndon remains on the periphery of Alabama's non-concert operations. A session drummer performs on the albums. And his only writing contribution to the first five RCA albums is coauthorship on "I'm Not That Way Anymore."

However, if the Alabama organization treats him as fairly as it does much lower-level employees, Herndon has a lot to be grateful for. And by all accounts, he is.

"I wanted to play more than anything else in my life," Herndon told Barry Bronson. "I used to go to concerts and just eat my heart out. I used to come home, get on my knees and just beg for it."

Bill Scroggins

CHAPTER 2

THE EARLY YEARS

If any one thing can be pointed to as the taproot of Alabama's professional triumphs, it is the fact that the band has stuck together through good times and bad. It is, as its members like to stress, a band "built to last." Except for the periodic rotation of the drummer's position, Alabama is the same mixture of personnel it was in 1969 when Randy Owen, Teddy Gentry, and Jeff Cook first got together to jam and sing—as much out of curiosity and a sense of fun as it was of ambition to make it in the music business.

Passion for music in the rural South is as common as sliced tomatoes. But nobody expects you to make a living at it. It's something you do after work and on weekends. So when this trio of cousins persisted in airing their musical dreams through high school, college, and straight into adulthood, more than one head around Fort Payne started shaking in disapproval at such a pitiful display of folly. Weren't these boys old enough to know better? Didn't they realize it was high time to settle down into real jobs? Couldn't they see there wasn't any future in playing in those old beer joints and shaming the folks who had tried to make good Christians out of them? Well, some things you've just got to learn for yourself, agreed the head-shakers, and the time would surely come when the boys would see the error of their ways.

These reactions—whether spoken aloud or merely hinted at—bound the cousins closer together. You can endure criticism better when there is someone else around to share it, and you can fight back harder with someone at your side to shout encouragement.

Teddy capsulized what it was like when he told a reporter: "I had a lady, a close friend of mine, tell me that I should get out of the music business, that she'd help me get a job at Wendy's and settle down. Four or five years ago, when I was approaching my mid-20s, I asked myself could I ask my family to depend on music for their livelihood. We finally got our turn. By us sticking together, everybody else wound up being wrong. Now they say we were right to do it this way."

Succeeding is always the best revenge.

BEGINNINGS

Professionally, the group's success story started in July, 1972, when they began working as the band-in-residence at Canyonland Park near Fort Payne. In this capacity, they not only entertained in their own right but also did the backup work for "name acts" booked in to increase the summer crowds. But Canyonland was to be a short interlude. Cook, Gentry, and Owen had heard of what seemed a far better venue to play than this out-of-the-way tourist park. Their musician friends in Fort Payne had said—and they believed them—that the real money to be made was in a rowdy oceanside bar in Myrtle Beach, South Carolina. And so, less than a year after their Canyonland debut, the three cousins hauled their instruments and dreams to the Bowery.

THE BOWERY

Stand on the wire-littered stage of the Bowery in Alabama's shoes and look out on the tightrope world you have created for yourself here in the early 1970s. Clear from your throat and nostrils the smoke of a hundred casually held and a thousand carelessly dropped cigarettes. Smell the tap beer sloshing onto the tabletops and running in zigzags across the sandy floor. Listen (as if you could do otherwise) to the hum, yelp, cackle, and groan of that erratic animal called "the crowd" that you have been dared to amuse and keep at bay.

Chairs scrape back and topple. Glasses clink. Greetings and taunts crisscross the damp, dark room, launched from remote corners. Tanned arms wave and beckon like seaweed. Heads tilt together as lies and legends are spread through straight young teeth.

Bartenders, taxed by the demands of communal thirsts, lose their tempers and snap at the timid and reluctantly innocent kids who stand around—kids who hope that someone will say hello or invite them to sit at their tables, maybe even take them by the hand and lead them out onto the beach for a night of love.

Older vacationers dart their heads through the open doors like curious chickens and quickly withdraw in relief, concluding that here, at least, is one tourist spot they can forgo in good conscience. The girl carrying the tip bucket weaves through an obstacle course of legs—table and human—and smiles up at you, brave victims acknowledging each other in this common storm. All this is swirling around you as you lean into your microphone, smiling automatically. It hits you again that, to this crowd, you're just a jukebox set on "free play."

If you're a party animal—as Jeff Cook is—you grin and stomp and eat it all up. You know the licks that'll make 'em twist and shout. You know that your guitar strings reach out like puppet wires to those fine young limbs, pulling them toward you. Another tug and you tilt those glorious heads and focus those speculating eyes. You are the A-1, certified boogie king of this grubby throne room until the doors slam shut at one o'clock. And even when those young bodies stumble out into the night with someone else, it doesn't matter—because nothing on land or water comes close to touching the music you've just been making.

If you're Randy Owen, fresh out of college with an English degree and your mind popping with all those damnably apt literary allusions, you might recall what they said about Willy Loman in *Death of a Sales-*

Photo courtesy of Joe Taylor

An early publicity photo of Wildcountry. Seated at left is Bennett Vartanian, drummer for the group from 1973 through early 1976. A diminutive Jeff Cook sits at right.

Alabama playing at the Bowery in 1979.

Bill Scroggins

man, because whatever else you and your band might be here on stage tonight—musicians, clowns, love objects—you are still salesmen above all: "He's a man out there in the blue, riding on a smile and a shoeshine." Well, this is pretty much what it's come to for all of you, Mr. Owen, except that you are out here, riding on a smile and a song. And if the crowd doesn't keep buying you, you can't keep buying the groceries and paying the rent.

That's the most beautifully instructive thing about picking just for tips—it teaches you to give the people what they want when they ask for it. That means you've got to know a lot of songs and be damn good at doing them, or it's back to the factory or farm. No delivery, no collection. Any salesman can tell you how crucial that little axiom is.

When you're an ominously quiet Teddy Gentry, staring at the kaleidoscopic movements of the crowd in front of you, you think how much better this is—at its worst—than laying carpet or sweating in your grandfather's hillside cotton patch under the indifferent brow of Lookout Mountain.

Watching those rich kids out in the audience, coming on to each other and spending Daddy's money, you can take some satisfaction in being absolutely sure that you're tougher and smarter and more adaptable now than they'll ever be. But you save these thoughts for quieter times. Right now, somebody out there is clamoring for "Proud Mary" again, and, hell, you just did it half an hour ago.

Looking through Gentry's eyes, always attuned to that bottom line, you wonder, though, how long you and your cousins can go on making only $100 or $200 a week apiece. And touring around the rest of the country in a van during the off-season is about as financially shaky as this beach gig. Sometimes it's worse. But there are a lot of folks out there, romping to your music. Maybe they'd buy your records, too, if you could ever get an album cut.

"Proud Mary" finished for the second of five times tonight, you look over at Jeff, nod and begin hammering out the beat for "Today I Started Loving You Again."

No matter whose eyes you looked through, you saw in the Bowery audiences a microcosm of a varied and demanding world. There could not have been a better training ground.

So how do you fortify yourself to withstand the rigors of such an unrelenting night scene? You practice your licks and harmonies until you know beyond doubt that, even in the face of the loudest criticisms and the most obnoxiously drunken request, you are good. Real good. Much better, in fact, than a roaring crowd will ever be able to appreciate. You choose the songs that work on stage because of their appeal to rhythm or for their unerring emotional hooks. You keep adding to your repertoire as if you're cramming for final exams, since any one of these nightly tests might be your last if you fail the crowd. You program yourself with so many lyrics and melodies and styles that you know you can upstage any jukebox in the universe.

Then, during those slim hours and days off, you speed away from the Bowery to the recording studios and publishing houses of Muscle Shoals or Nashville to chase the bits of dreams that have survived the night before. If there is any time left, maybe then you can pursue those personal relationships you make your living singing about so convincingly. When you're too tired to do anything else, you turn on the radio and learn another song for the crowd.

Melodie Gimple

CHAPTER 3

ON THE CHARTS: NASHVILLE

Oere it was—another irresistible song springing up from Alabama roots, and at least half of America was singing along with it like new converts at a revival meeting. When that many people are singing along, cash registers at record stores are humming, too. So *Billboard* magazine was right there on the spot to chronicle the parade of dollar signs. Anytime there's a buck to be made in the music business, *Billboard* leaps to explain just how it's done.

The song *Billboard* was reporting on this fine midsummer day was Jimmy Buffett's ode to the tropical good life, "Margaritaville." A son of the port city of Mobile, Alabama, Buffett had been scratching at the door of success for years before anyone took much notice of him. "Margaritaville" simply knocked that door off its hinges. By July, 1977, Buffett had clearly arrived—windblown, suntanned, and solvent.

With so much hoopla about Buffett to attend to, the magazine's readers could be forgiven if they failed to notice a timid new entry onto the "Hot Country Singles" chart printed on the back of the Buffett story. Edging in at the bottom of the list—precisely at No. 100, the lowest spot—was a song called "I Wanna Be with You Tonight." It was recorded by a new act that had apparently taken its name from Buffett's home state. The act was calling itself "Alabama."

THE FIRST SINGLE

Although GRT Records, on which "I Wanna Be with You Tonight" made its bow, was a small independent label, it was no innocent in the music industry. At that moment, GRT could point to the charts at some extremely encouraging action taking place under its banner. Alabama had reasons to be hopeful about its own recording future. Meri Wilson's naughty novelty, "Telephone Man," had broken into the top 50, and Johnny Lee's cover treatment of Ricky Nelson's "Garden Party" ("Country Party") was at number 15. Both were GRT projects.

In February, 1977, transplanted Pennsylvanian Scott Tutt signed Wildcountry to a management contract in which the group conceded that it would change its name for recording purposes and in which Tutt guaranteed he would get them a chart record or else release them from their contract. He then proceeded to produce "I Wanna Be with You Tonight" on a very tight budget. Then all he had to do was take the results of the session and convince a record label to sign the act.

What could be more natural, Tutt asked himself, than pitching the act to his former employers at GRT? "The reason we got them on GRT," Tutt later recounted, "was that we had a little party to play the music for Tom McEntee [who was then national promotion director for the label]. He didn't know we'd specially planned this evening. We had in fact set it up so that nobody else would sit in the chair we had between the speakers. That seat was purposely left vacant so McEntee would have the best seat in the room. It all worked out. He liked the song so much he kept asking us to play it again. So we had an ace in the hole when we then pitched the master [recording] to Dick Heard," head of GRT's Nashville office.

The Trials of Record Promotion

As soon as GRT took the record, sent it back to the studio for a little sweetening, and then released it, Tutt hit the road to promote the record to radio stations. Because self-contained bands were rare in country music, Tutt says he sometimes identified his new act as "Randy Owen and Alabama." "They hated this," Tutt recalls. "Randy didn't like it, either. Randy at the time was very, very shy, although not on stage. He could take charge on stage, but he was not a leader. He was not really the quarterback of the team, and he should have been. He was the most educated, and he was the one everybody felt was the superstar."

Tutt put all his promotional imagination into the cause. Even before the single was shipped to radio stations, he sent them a specially designed "teaser" sheet that said "COMING SOON! . . . the looks in your eyes keep saying 'I WANNA BE WITH YOU TONIGHT' by ALABAMA." The teaser showed the picture of a sultry dark-haired woman whose eyes reflected the tune's title. The same artwork was then used on the single sleeve, a connection Tutt hoped radio programmers would remember. Karen Green, the woman who posed for the pic-

ture, even did some station visits to promote the record.

Although GRT was less than lavish in the promotion budget it assigned to the new record, Tutt did raise enough money to give Alabama a party to celebrate the release of the single. Appropriately, the party was held at the Bowery at noon on Saturday, June 11. A month later, Tutt made good his promise of getting the record on the charts.

But getting the song there and keeping it climbing were two different matters, he learned. For three straight weeks, the song stayed at number 100—the musical equivalent of neither being fully alive nor totally dead. So perilous was the record's condition that Tutt decided he might get some mileage by joking with radio about it. To that end, he and McEntee created a "Golden 100 Club" award for GRT, noting mischievously that "it takes just the right combination of stations adding the record and those who are 'watching it' to maintain such a delicate balance." The award would be presented, they deadpanned, "at a special ceremony to be held behind Nashville's Wax Museum."

Whether this desperation move made a difference or not isn't clear. But something happened, and "I Wanna Be with You Tonight" began picking up stations and slowly climbing the charts.

"When I was on the promotion trip," Tutt remembers, "I had been out there about five days, and I was beat and grouchy and I wanted to come home. I didn't know if I wanted to be in the record business anymore. Pulling into Savannah—I had all the numbers of the radio stations—I punched the button up on the radio station, tuned it in and [the DJ] said, 'Here's a new song by a

GRT RECORDS AND THE BOWERY
REQUEST THE PLEASURE OF YOUR COMPANY AT THE
SIGNING PARTY FOR THE COUNTRY/ROCK BAND,
ALABAMA.
THE DATE OF THE PARTY IS SATURDAY,
JUNE 11th, JUST PRIOR TO THE RELEASE OF
THEIR FIRST SINGLE ON GRT RECORDS,
"I WANNA BE WITH YOU TONIGHT".

PLACE: "THE BOWERY"
9th AVENUE NORTH & OCEAN BLVD.
MYRTLE BEACH, S.C.
DATE: JUNE 11th, 1977
TIME: 12 NOON
FEEL FREE TO BRING A GUEST

RECORDS & TAPES

GRT RECEIVES

"GOLDEN 100 CLUB" AWARD

With the record-breaking chart activity of Alabama's "I WANNA BE WITH YOU TONIGHT", GRT Records will receive the Golden 100 Club Award, given to records that maintain a minimum of 3 weeks at the 100 spot on any trade chart. The Alabama record becomes the first entry into the new club, and, as such, will receive the coveted "Anchor" award at a special ceremony to be held behind Nashville's Wax Museum later this week.

"Holding the No.100 position for 3 straight weeks is no small feat", comments the label's national promotion director, Tom McEntee. "It takes just the right combination of stations adding the record and those who are "watching it" to maintain such a delicate balance". Unfortunately, a great many of the music directors who have been "watching" the record have complained of boredom and are contemplating adding it to their playlists. As a result we may move up from our present position and, of course, lose our opportunity to set still further records for keeping a lock on the 100 spot.

* * * * * * * * * * *

P.S. New adds this week include:

KCEY - Turlock
KFDI - Wichita
KEBC - Oklahoma City
WDEN - Macon
WQCK - Warner Robbins
WJQS - Jackson
WKYG - Parkersburg
KRDR - Gresham, OR

GRT Records • 1226 16th Avenue South • Nashville, Tennessee 37212 • (615) 383-0800

group called Alabama.' And as soon as the record came on, I was ready to go on the road for another six months."

Management Difficulties

Even with a taste of success, the band members did not gracefully accept their new name. Tutt kept telling them it was a great name, like "Boston" or "Chicago." They finally did agree, but they still had material printed up that said "Alabama Band" on it.

"It was tough working with a group that had managed itself for years," Tutt contends. "All of a sudden they had to OK things. . . . Like every band starting out, they always 'had a friend.' As we were getting the T-shirt logo ready to go, they jumped the gun and got some friend of theirs to draw a close resemblance of the logo. And they printed it on these T-shirts that, if you washed them once, they became a child's size T-shirt. For a quarter more, they could have gotten the best T-shirt with a super print job. They just jumped the gun on a lot of things—and those were the kinds of things that, being a manager in Nashville with your band in Myrtle Beach, you couldn't control."

Problems with the band, problems with a faltering GRT, and problems with a record that had climbed as high as it was going to go all conspired to put an end to the Alabama-Tutt relationship. Besides, Tutt swears, he was simply unable to make a living concentrating on Alabama's career.

By his account, he had concluded near the end of his year with the band that it was time to part company. As payment for his services, he says, Alabama gave him the publishing rights to four of their songs, including such later hits as "Tennessee River" and "Lady Down on Love."

And there was another complication to ending the contract, Tutt admits: "I've seen it in print that they had to pay money to get out of their contract [with me]. Yes, they did. I required them to pay me $800 that they owed me, and I said, 'You're free.' If that's selling an act, I sold them back to themselves for $800. What they leave out [of their stories about management woes] is the $800 figure. I said, 'Boys, I will let you go, but you will pay me for the 8 × 10s you've got on sale. You'll pay me for the T-shirts we did'—that type of stuff we put our money into to sell at their gigs."

But in spite of the soured relationship, Tutt still praises his one-time clients: "The one thing about the boys was perseverance. They were willing to do anything. *Anything!* I mean anybody who is willing to play from seven o'clock to midnight without a break is willing to do anything. If they had been told they could move along a year in their career if they stood on their heads and played their instruments every night, they would have learned how to do that. They really believed that one day they were going to be big stars. I didn't believe all this was going to happen. I believed we could put records on the charts. I believed we could entertain a crowd, and that with a few breaks we might do all right. A realistic approach. Their approach was, 'We're gonna be as big as Conway Twitty.' "

If Alabama studied and exclaimed over its first inclusion on the charts—as most fledgling acts do—it probably noticed that rockabilly stylist Billy "Crash" Craddock was in the No. 10 spot on *Billboard*'s weekly survey with "A Tear Fell." Craddock had been a major country act since 1971, when he grabbed a few million ears with "Knock Three Times." He owed much of his success to the aid of a former pharmaceutical salesman named Dale Morris. It was on Morris's tiny Cartwheel label that Craddock scored with "Knock Three Times." Later Morris would become his manager and later still—near the end of the '70s—the two would establish the booking agency International House of Talent. Like random weather patterns that swirl in together to spawn a tornado, the Craddock-Morris mixture

Vernell Hackett

would sweep Alabama—many years later—into one of the costliest and most frustrating legal storms in the group's unusually stormy existence.

BACK TO THE BOWERY

For a number of reasons, money problems and more interest in its better-known artists being the chief ones, GRT Records in late 1977 was unable to write a happy ending to the dream it had started for the Fort Payne foursome. After several dispiriting weeks on the charts, "I Wanna Be with You Tonight" sluggishly inched its way up to number 77 and then dropped with a noise that must have sounded like a heart breaking. A month after Alabama broke into the charts, Elvis Presley died, and Ronnie McDowell immediately recorded the memorial "The King Is Gone" for Scorpion Records. The song was an instant hit, but because Scorpion was too small to manufacture and distribute a real hit record, GRT took over those tasks. Thus, it had even less time and money to waste on the young strugglers from Fort Payne. Well, they must have consoled themselves, an act could do a lot worse than settle in as the most famous bar band in Myrtle Beach, and it was to this limited prospect that Alabama again turned its weary attention.

Encouraged at what they had achieved and smarting over what they hadn't, the boys spent the following year making music and plans. Once the initial disappointment ebbed at not going higher on the charts, the group could still take comfort in knowing that they had stayed on longer and climbed up farther than most first-time entrants. And while the learning hadn't been all that pretty, they had certainly learned a lot about how the complex music business operates.

In 1978, Alabama celebrated its fifth anniversary at the Bowery. Then, early the next year, longtime drummer Rick Scott, who had built his own following while working with Alabama and who already shared several songwriting credits with the group,

Alabama on stage.

Melodie Gimple

Jim Rawlings

Mark Herndon: the last to join the band.

decided to leave the band. He was the fifth or sixth stickman to do so, and each departure caused the remaining three to wonder—at least momentarily—if theirs was the right business to stay in. As Jeff Cook later explained to reporter Vernell Hackett, "Every time a drummer quit, you had to come back in and teach the new man all the stuff you'd been playing for the last five or six years. . . . It's as much work to teach the fourth person as it is to learn the songs from scratch."

Nonetheless, a group that had come this far could hardly chuck it all for good without making another try at stability. So in March of 1979, the boys auditioned Mark Herndon. He passed their inspection and officially came on board April 1.

BREAKTHROUGH

Having gotten their musical house back in order, Alabama decided to launch another foray into the record business, this time with the song "I Wanna Come Over." It was issued first on the Limbo International label (a name that roughly translates into "Nowhere Everywhere"). Happily, the name was not prophetic, because the recording executive Larry McBride chanced to hear the record, a joy few others at the time had experienced, and offered to reissue and promote it under his own MDJ Records logo. In this regard, McBride was as good as his word. What Alabama didn't realize at the time was that, only a year before, McBride had been convicted of conspiracy and wire fraud.

"I Wanna Come Over" entered the *Billboard* country charts September 29, 1979, and stayed there for three months. During that time it rose to number 33, quite a respectable showing, even if all had ended there.

On the strength of its chart action and boosted by McBride's passion for promotion, Alabama earned itself a spot on the important New Faces showcase that was scheduled to be held as part of the Country Radio Seminar in Nashville in March, just a few weeks after the excitement of the record's chart achievement was dying down. The Country Radio Seminar is an institution that testifies to the truth that modern radio broadcasting is more a business than an art. Its purpose is primarily to educate the general managers, program directors, and music directors of radio stations on how to do their work more profitably. Amidst its heavy hours of instruction, however, it allows for the introduction of a few delights. And one of these is the annual New Faces show.

Aside from its purely entertainment function, the purpose of the show is to introduce to country radio's decision-makers the acts whose records their stations will be or should be playing. Given the influence of the audience, record companies naturally clamor for their new acts to be exposed to the elite group. Not just the small labels, but the major ones as well, jockey to get their nominees past the Seminar's selection committee. Once an act has been selected, the label must still pay the Seminar a fee for the act's right to appear.

All this being the case, it was a considerable victory when McBride got his young charges accepted. They would, he told them, make their debut to the broadcasters on the evening of March 15, 1980, in the cavernous Regency Ballroom of the Hyatt Regency Hotel in downtown Nashville. This would be the eleventh annual Seminar, and its theme was phrased precisely to indicate drama without promising anything dramatic: "Answers for the '80s."

For all the show's supposed significance, the New Faces selectors have been only mildly prescient about the talent they present. Some acts, as Alabama would amply demonstrate, do, indeed, go on to great things. But many New Faces gain little more celebrity than that which they enjoyed on the occasion of their showcasing. This dismal fact has less to do with the selectors' ears for talent than it does with such fatal variables as lack of commitment on the part of the label or the artist, the enormous cost of launching an artist, or the fickleness of the marketplace.

The other acts selected to appear with Alabama on the showcase were Big Al Downing, Leon Everette, Lacy J. Dalton, Sylvia, Juice Newton, Carol Chase, Jim Weatherly, and Reba McEntire. To cut down on the number of applicants for New Faces, the Seminar had just this year added the stipulation that only acts that had charted in the top 50 of *Billboard*, *Cash Box*, or *Record World* would be considered. There was another first this year, too, that testified to McBride's persuasiveness: for the first time the show would have a band (and not just solo acts) in the lineup.

Melodie Gimple

The high-ceilinged and thickly carpeted Regency Ballroom was nothing like the grubby, airless, sandy-floored confines of the Bowery, a fact that did not distress Cook, Owen, Gentry, and Herndon in the least. Nor, after seven years of playing for loud and drunken college students, was there any nervousness at the prospect of performing to a banquet of randomly loud and only mildly drunken radio and music executives. What did upset the boys—even infuriate them—was discovering that they would not be allowed to back themselves with their own instruments. The Seminar had hired some of the best studio musicians in town to do that.

So Mark Herndon got to celebrate his first anniversary with the band by sitting in the audience and watching Buddy Harman pound out his part. And Owen, Gentry, and Cook had to show their stuff while clutching at microphones like desperate lounge singers instead of wielding their guitars like the seasoned musicians they had long since become. But the worst of it, as the group remembers and as unbiased witnesses swear to, was that the backup band seemed to be dozing through its paces. Reviewing the show for *Billboard*, writer Kip Kirby noted that the show placed "a heavy emphasis on pop" and only "a modicum on what used to be called traditional country." And the acts, she added, "displayed high degrees of professionalism and unbridled enthusiasm on stage." The same could not be said, she observed, of the backup musicians who "acted as though they'd rather be anywhere else." Continued Kirby, "Some yawned and sat like bored statues, dragging the pace and apparently relying on their reputations and studio smugness. This sleepy, uninspired approach to the show's music was put to shame by the fresh vibrancy of the artists they were supposedly showcasing."

Of the nine acts, Kirby judged that the "obvious favorites were songs by Juice Newton, Alabama, Big Al Downing, and Lacy J. Dalton."

Alabama was pictured twice in the Seminar program: once in the two-page New Faces layout and again in a full-page ad. In both places, the group was identified as "The Alabama." And in both places, the same publicity photo was used. Owen and Gentry looked about the same then as they do now. But Herndon had shoulder-length hair instead of the spiked punk style he later favored. Moreover, he was grinning to please, a pose he would soon enough abandon in preference to a stony-faced smirk. The pictures are indistinct, but Herndon seems to be sporting just a trace of a beard. Guitar wizard Jeff Cook, his paunch several hundred snacks smaller than it has since become, also affects the shoulder-length cut and is even wearing suitably rural suspenders.

Larry McBride was pleased at the attention his new act was getting; soon after the New Faces debut, McBride signed Alabama to an exclusive recording contract with his record label and then compounded his hold on the band by signing it to a management contract with him. Because a small label generally lacks the resources to get its records distributed and promoted no matter how good its acts are, it is common in the music business for the small label to link itself to a larger one. The small label will keep a "piece" of the act, figuring that it is more profitable to have part of a huge act than all of a tiny one. In pursuit of this notion, on April 11, barely a month after the New Faces show, McBride signed over Alabama to the corporate mercies and marketing genius of RCA Records. He retained his rights as manager of the group.

Looking back on this pivotal period in Alabama's professional life, one concludes that McBride must have been signing documents with the same intensity and glee as that with which Alabama was making music. The document McBride signed on May 22 is one that still haunts Alabama. On that day, he signed the Fort Payne Four to an exclusive three-year booking contract with Billy "Crash" Craddock and Dale Morris's International House of Talent. And he gave IHT the option to renew for another three years what would become the biggest booking bonanza in country music.

Larry Dixon

CHAPTER

4

THE RIGHT TIME AND THE RIGHT ACT

The members of Alabama are tiresomely fond of telling interviewers that if they knew what the formula for success was they would bottle it. Well, they do know. They know it's simply a matter of becoming very good at your trade and then sticking with it while your competition prays for luck and looks for shortcuts.

Fundamental to Alabama's wide appeal has been its patiently crafted ability to cover all musical bases. If record and ticket buyers lust for slick L.A. pop, then just trot out those polished Eagles-like vocal harmonies (with appropriately cosmic love themes, of course) and wait for the cheers. If the crowd wants traditional country, tell the drummer to hold it down a speck, let Randy sing solo, and hand Jeff his fiddle. If they cry out for "Amazing Grace" on one of those awful nights when you are neither amazed by it nor sure of its existence, bring out those four-part harmonies you learned some thousand Sunday mornings back and let all your pains and frustrations pour through.

WHY IS ALABAMA SO POPULAR?

It should in no way diminish the group's accomplishments to observe that Alabama probably succeeded by being in the right place at the right time—for, as any statistician will confirm, your chances for success are vastly improved if you're in a lot of different places at a lot of different times—in other words, if you work hard and stay at it, which is clearly Alabama's specialty.

Although the band couldn't have known it, the world that would eventually be toasting them started taking a new shape in the mid-'70s. Its television cameras having been chased out of Vietnam along with its troops, America started paying more attention to

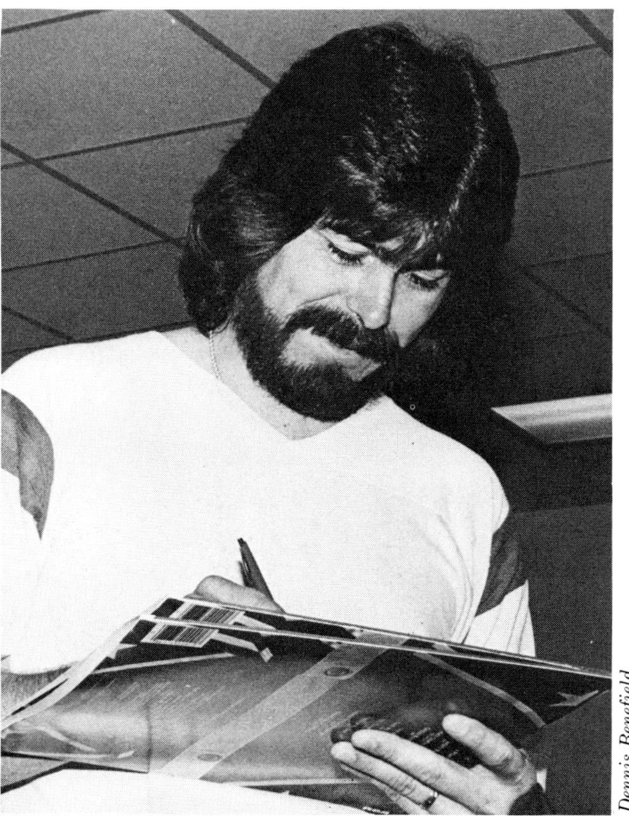
Dennis Benefield

what was happening within its own borders. A specific result of this refocusing was, of course, the around-the-clock coverage of the Watergate fallout. But a more general effect of bringing the cameras home was to turn our attention inward—to make us less the "global villagers" and world citizens we thought we had become in the '60s and to confine us again to being just "American villagers." We were media-nudged, ever so gradually, toward adopting that fortress mentality that has for so many years been considered, rightly or wrongly, a peculiarly Southern outlook—the us-against-them perspective.

Celebration of the South

In due time, the kind of social provincialism the media had specialized in exposing and diluting when it was just a Southern quality became quite respectable as a national one. Religious and political opinions so old-fashioned that they would have been laughed out of the television studios in the '60s became matters of serious coverage and debate on the six o'clock network news by the mid-'70s.

Viewed as a mild, if necessary, irritant in the '60s, one's family started becoming a source of strength and pride ten years later. Thanks to the fireworks over Alex Haley's *Roots*, people who had formerly become nauseous at the thought of certain first cousins were suddenly scrambling to remote courthouses to find out minutiae about great-grandfather.

With neither the threat of a military draft to radicalize them nor the prospect of plentiful jobs to make them smug, American youth seemed to conclude that the '70s was the decade to play it safe and not rattle any cages.

Old-time religion. Insularity. Attachment to family. Cautiousness. Where had these basic traits of conservatism been incubating and thriving all along? Not in New York and on "All in the Family." Not in Los Angeles and in the quest for *est*. No, sir, these good things were on parade Down South and being celebrated, as ever, in country music.

Within a mere ten years, the South had been transformed from the Dogpatch of the Western World into the Fort Knox of American Values. How else could a man who boasted of being a "born again" Christian and who talked like an escapee from the cast of *Gone with the Wind* end up being elected president of the United States?

So it came to pass that while Wildcountry/Alabama was down there in Myrtle Beach sharpening its act with every drunken request shouted to it, much of the rest of the nation had decided (or was deciding) that it was OK to be Southern. Maybe even cool.

Jimmy Carter did not turn out to be a particularly popular leader, but like all leaders he got massive coverage. Plains, Georgia, in all its rural quaintness, became a suburb of wherever it was that the rest of us

Courtesy of Jacksonville State University

Alabama holds a pre-concert press conference.

lived. And not just the president, but his press secretary, his cabinet officers, his advisers, and his friends acclimated us to the "Southern English" Randy Owen defended in "My Home's in Alabama." But as important as any of these incidental influences were, even more significant was the fact that Carter announced to all who would hear that he loved country music. And he proceeded to demonstrate that point by inviting country stars to the White House by the busload. One of Carter's more frequent callers was Willie Nelson, who was already doing his bit to cultivate a seedbed in which groups like Alabama might flourish.

Willie Nelson

More than anyone else, Nelson can take the credit for bringing young people into country music. In his small, bearded, and blissfully smiling personage, he seemed to embody rebel, guru, best friend, and understanding daddy. He was macho without being menacing. He was literate without being literary. And for years he was on more magazine covers than the bar code.

The laboratory in which this Texas alchemist fused the Northern and Southern cultures and transplanted the results into the old head he had grafted onto a young body was his series of Fourth of July Picnics. And doesn't that sound All-American, down home, and family? The first one was held in 1972. These outdoor concerts had enough of a rock festival air about them to draw young people by the thousands. What they saw, in addition to the eternal Willie, was some pretty traditional country picking. Wonder of wonders, many found they liked it.

While Nelson was luring the youth of America toward music with his picnics, he was also slyly beckoning to the older, pop-oriented audiences to lean back and listen to his albums—particularly *Stardust.* This collection of standards was sufficiently smooth, melodic, and sentimental to clutch the soft hearts and hardened arteries of even Frank Sinatra fans. But there was still Nelson's obviously country voice doing the interpreting. That Nelson knew what he was shooting for in *Stardust* is evident by the fact that it has been on the bestselling

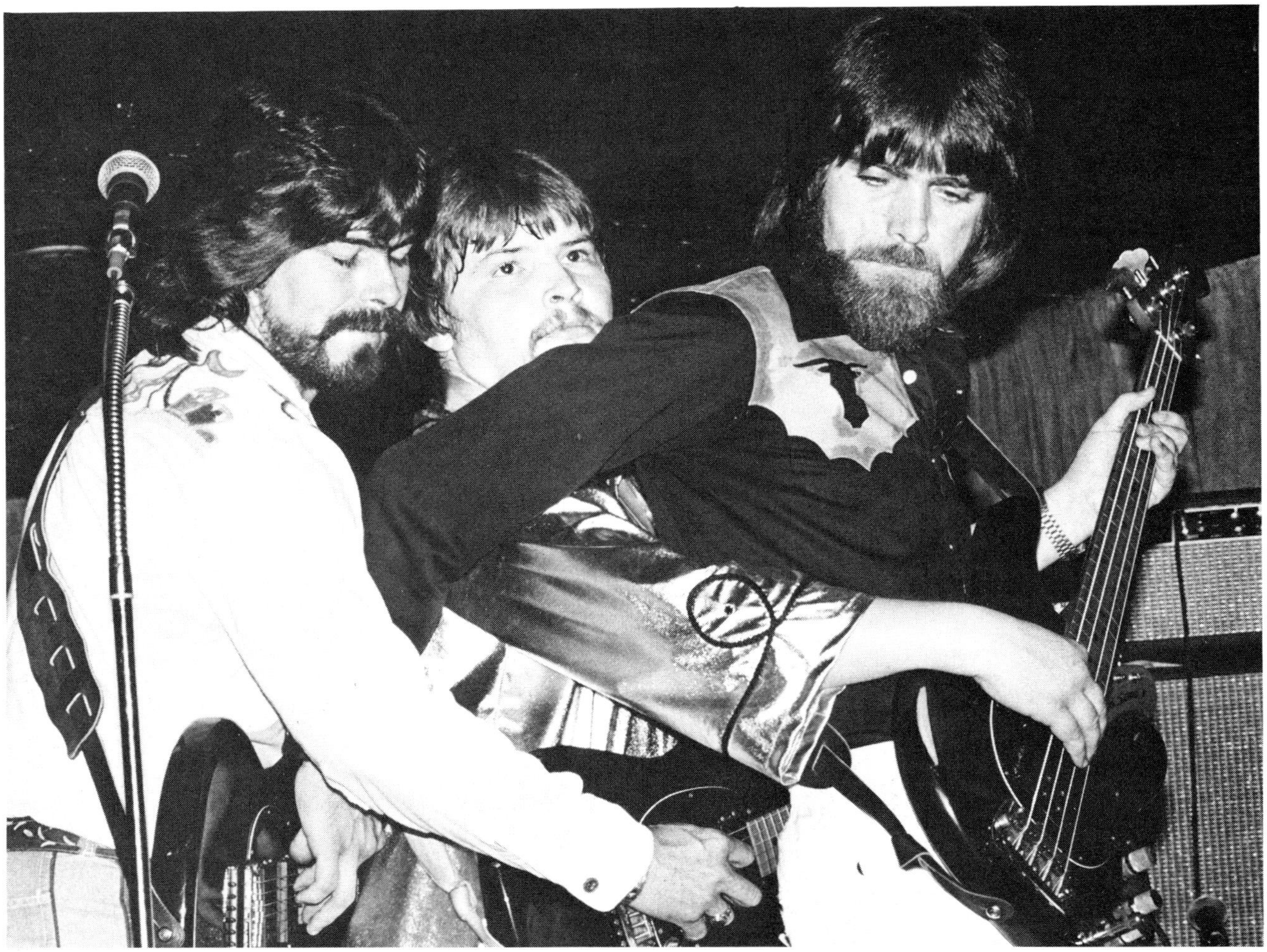

Melodie Gimple

"Now you fret and I'll pick—and I'll fret while you pick."

country album chart for more than six years.

Whether Nelson was leading a rock-oriented youngster toward George Jones via his picnic or a big-band fan toward Lefty Frizzell through his albums, he was beating the drum to get people to come over to country music who had never liked nor considered it before. And from this movement Alabama was destined to benefit.

Charlie Daniels was also doing his part during the '70s to extend country music's borders. In 1974, he instituted the Volunteer Jam, an all-night indoor concert that mixed rock, bluegrass, cajun, country, and (at least once) even classical music performances together in happy indifference to style. Moreover, Daniels's own hit songs, such as "The South's Gonna Do It Again," "Long-Haired Country Boy," and "The Devil Went Down to Georgia," spread more good words about Dixie.

Even the Oak Ridge Boys, whose career absolutely soared following the 1977 release of "Y'All Come Back Saloon," acclimated radio programmers and concert promoters to the boundless possibilities a tight country vocal group could offer.

Television and Movies

In 1976, when it appeared that Austin, Texas, was going to be the country/rock music mecca hometowners were predicting it would be, the Public Broadcasting System (PBS) introduced "Austin City Limits"

Continued on page 54.

FANS OF THE BAND

Larry Dixon

Larry Dixon

All photos by Larry Dixon

THE RIGHT TIME AND THE RIGHT ACT

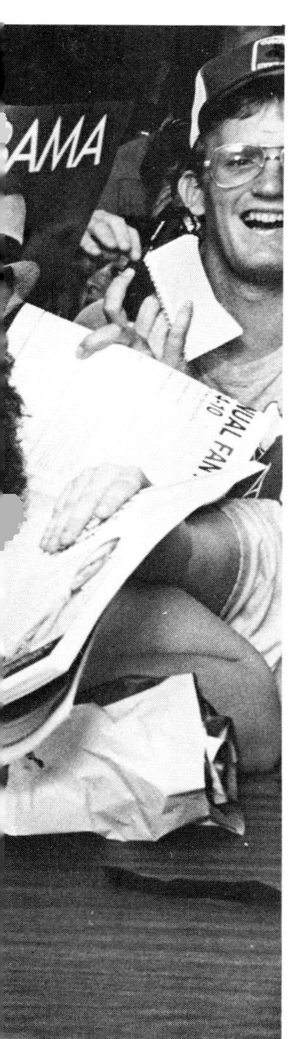

Dedicated fans have made Alabama one of the hottest concert tickets in the country and the members of the band are dedicated to please them. At left, Randy Owen literally bends over backward to give a fan a special souvenir, while (below right) Jeff Cook gives a fan an excuse not to take a shower. On this page, Mark Herndon bends over, too, to sign autographs, while Teddy Gentry works on his own case of writer's cramp.

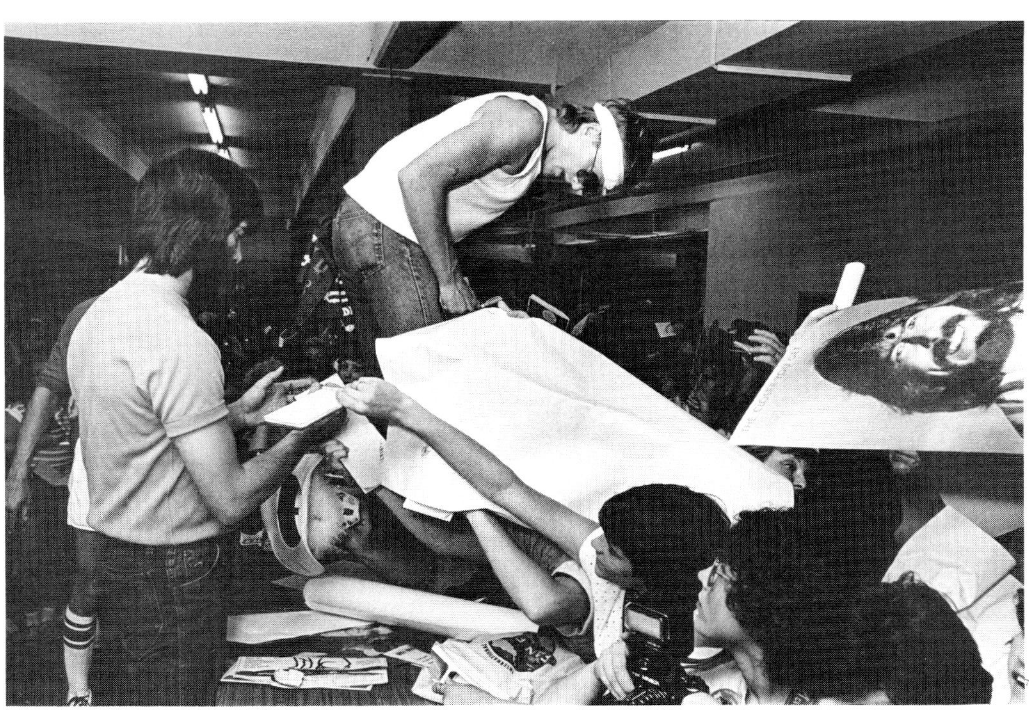

Continued from page 50.

to its lineup, a modest enough move, but one that again brought country or quasi-country music to more unfamiliar ears. The response to this program was so great that PBS, in 1978, featured a live television broadcast of the Grand Ole Opry to draw viewers to its fund-raising period. This venture ensured that even more people who could not remember the difference between Roy Acuff and Roy Rogers would become acquainted with the alluring variety country music had to offer.

The market for Alabama was building.

Coal Miner's Daughter, the movie version of Loretta Lynn's life, premiered in March, 1980, and immediately established itself as the most intelligent and comprehensive film about country music ever made. No good-ole-boy epic (like Burt Reynolds's direct-to-drive-in efforts, for instance), *Coal Miner's Daughter* had the kind of acting and scripting that even intellectuals could exclaim about. And they did. The film was both a critical and a box office hit. The effect, again, was to make the country music world a part of the national consciousness. But it remained for *Urban Cowboy*, which opened three months later, to make the country fall in love with country music.

From a pure media point of view, *Urban Cowboy* had it all over *Coal Miner's Daughter*. *Daughter* had style, while *Cowboy* had fashions. In *Daughter*, the locations were background; in *Cowboy*, the location, Gilley's nightclub, was also one of the stars. *Daughter* celebrated maturity, and *Cowboy* touted youthful boisterousness. But the biggest difference—and the one from which Alabama would benefit most—was the variety of music that would be wedged into an ostensibly "country music" film. In *Coal Miner's Daughter* all the music was the kind you might hear on the Grand Ole Opry, which is to say traditional country music. But in *Urban Cowboy*, the sound track featured the likes of Boz Scaggs, Jimmy Buffett, Anne Murray, Linda Ronstadt and J. D. Souther, Bonnie Raitt, the Charlie Daniels Band, Mickey Gilley, and Johnny Lee.

Melodie Gimple

Stills for an album cover

The mixture was strong enough to send Gilley and Lee into the higher reaches of the

Melodie Gimple

Randy Owen gives an appreciative kiss on the cheek to Frances Preston, vice president of Broadcast Music, Inc.

pop charts with such entries as "Stand By Me," "True Love Ways," and "Lookin' for Love," while Raitt and Buffett got country airplay, via "Don't It Make You Wanna Dance" and "Hello Texas." By August 16, 1980, the week Alabama had its first number 1 hit with "Tennessee River," it took a team of scholars and a couple of astrologers to say just what was and wasn't a country song.

Jeff Cook concedes his group had the stars on its side: "It was a matter of timing. Movies like *Urban Cowboy* just did so much to make country music popular. We don't like to put a label on our music, but after that movie, everybody wanted country music." The right place, the right time, the right stuff.

CHAPTER 5
TROUBLE IN PARADISE

After Alabama signed with RCA Records in the spring of 1980, the band's good fortunes surged and spread like high water through a split dam. Less than two months after the signing, Alabama released its first RCA single "Tennessee River"—and its first RCA album—*My Home's in Alabama*.

On August 16, 1980, "Tennessee River" went to the top of *Billboard*'s country singles chart—just as virtually every other Alabama single would do for the next several years. But this accomplishment, being the first No. 1, must have been the sweetest. Before the year was out, "Why Lady Why" also went to the top. And in January, 1981, Alabama established its first fan club headquarters in Fort Payne.

Recognition was mounting in other quarters too. The Academy of Country Music—which is sort of the West Coast equivalent of the Country Music Association—got the jump on the CMA by being the first to cite Alabama on a nationally televised awards show. On April 30, 1981, the ACM proclaimed the Fort Payne Four "Vocal Group of the Year."

Less than four weeks after this happy event occurred, the Recording Industry Association of America (RIAA) announced that Alabama's *Feels So Right* album, which had been released in February, had gone "gold." That meant that the record had sold 500,000 copies—a phenomenal amount for a new group, and one which (according to rumor) RCA said it would be happy with if it sold 60,000 units during this early period. Then, in July, *My Home's in Alabama* reached gold status. The group that had struggled so long to sell a few hundred of its own albums had—within 15 months—sold a million for RCA. By September 15, 1981, *Feels So Right* earned the RIAA's "platinum" award for having sold a million units.

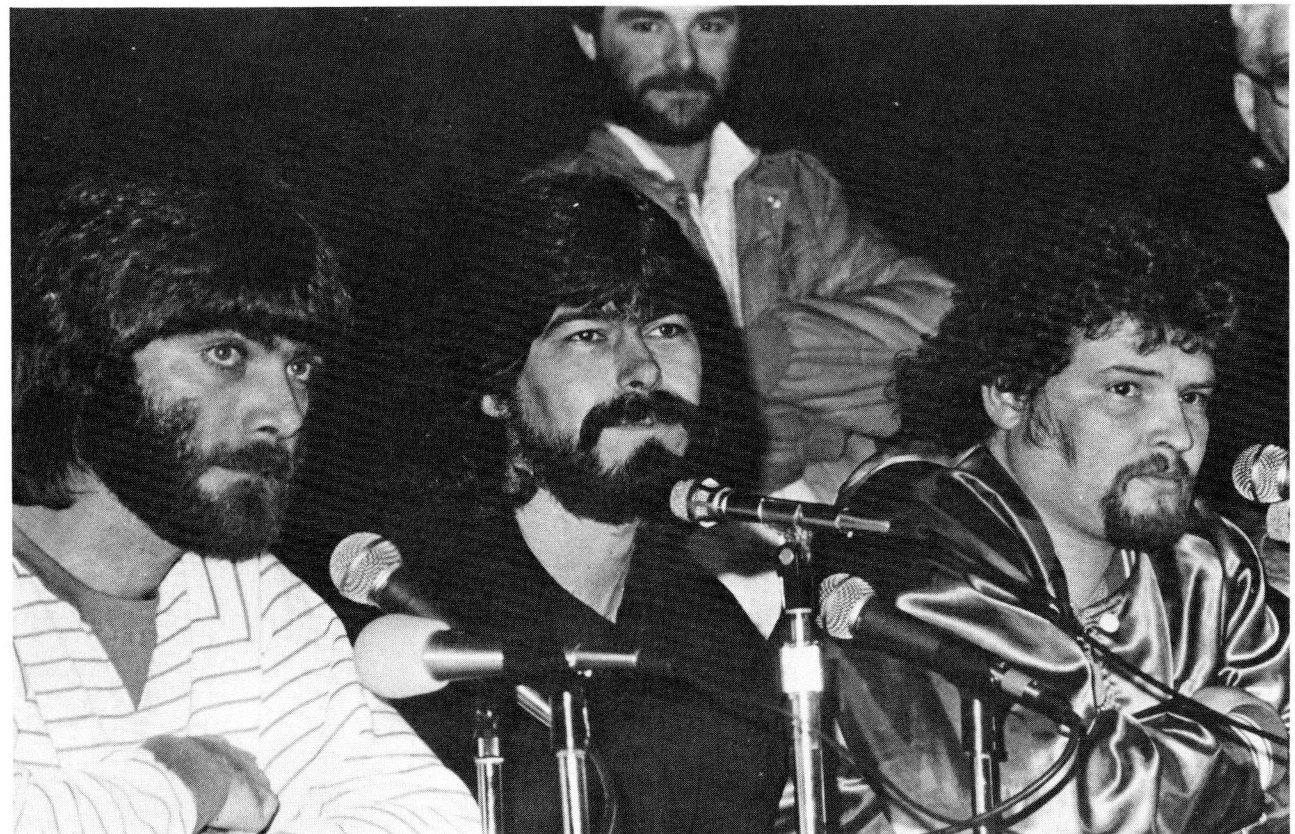
Dennis Benefield

Teddy, Randy, and Jeff ponder questions at a press conference, while their publicist, Greg Fowler, looks on.

The Country Music Association, which begins polling its membership in the summer to calculate its fall award winners, acknowledged in October that Alabama's star was, indeed, on the rise, by awarding the group its Instrumental Group and Vocal Group honors. During the next two years, Alabama almost seemed to have its own key to the closet where the CMA kept its awards.

With such enormous record sales and so many important awards cascading on the band, Alabama enjoyed a commensurate rise in its concert audiences. In 1980, Alabama was drawing a few hundred fans at each concert; now the band started pulling them in by the thousands.

One measure of Alabama's popularity was that the fan club had to move within a year to larger headquarters, and then move two more times within the next year—always to bigger buildings. Finally, the club took over an abandoned car dealership to give itself enough elbow room.

By 1982, Alabama had become full-fledged media darlings whose rags-to-royalty movement was being chronicled by journals great and small. That year, the ACM gave three prizes to the band: Vocal Group of the Year, Album of the Year (for *Feels So Right*) and—most significantly—Entertainer of the Year.

Mountain Music was released in February and proclaimed platinum by late April.

On June 4, Alabama held its first June Jam. The outdoor festival, which became an annual event, was held on the outskirts of Fort Payne to raise money for local charities. And even during this first year, it attracted tens of thousands of fans.

In February, 1983, the National Academy of Recording Arts and Sciences (NARAS) bestowed on the band its first Grammy. The prize, for the group's *Mountain Music*, read "Best Country Performance by a Duo or Group."

Alabama presents producer Harold Shedd a gold album for his production work on "Feels So Right."

Melodie Gimple

And again, Alabama won the ACM's Vocal Group and Entertainer of the Year honors. The CMA followed up these distinctions by presenting Alabama *its* Entertainer of the Year award for the second consecutive time, thereby matching Barbara Mandrell's record. Additionally, the band won awards as Vocal Group of the Year and for Album of the Year (*The Closer You Get*).

Professionally, Alabama was on top of the world. But such a string of financial success stories was bound to result in some spectacular and expensive legal hassles from those who wanted to share the group's new-found wealth. And the hassles did arrive.

LITIGATION BLUES

Since Alabama is involved in the earning and spending of such large sums of money, the group has been involved in constant litigation. Some observers say that, in addition to the lure caused by its riches, Alabama has attracted lawsuits by being naive about the ways of business. Early in the group's career it was certainly careless about safeguarding the rights to songs that would later become immensely valuable pieces of property.

An expensive error in judgment arose when Alabama broke a booking contract made by former manager Larry McBride. The agreement with Dale Morris—then president of International House of Talent—was signed May 22, 1980, a little more than a month after Alabama went with RCA Records. It gave Morris and/or IHT (depending on which version of the legal conflict you believe) the exclusive right to book the band for three years and the option to renew the contract for three more years.

During the next several months, Alabama split with McBride after learning that he was a convicted felon. Briefly, one of

Early in its association with RCA Records, Alabama poses with three of the men most important in its career: Larry McBride, third from left, president of MDJ Records and then the group's manager; Jerry Bradley, fifth from left, then head of RCA's Nashville branch; and Harold Shedd, extreme right, Alabama's producer.

McBride's associates, T. Howard Hamilton, stepped in as manager. Finally, in March 1981, Alabama voted to have Morris as manager. When the board of directors of IHT subsequently ousted Morris from the presidency, Morris formed his own company, independent from IHT, and took Alabama with him as a client.

On October 3, 1981, IHT sued Alabama for the 10 percent commission it estimated it would have earned had Alabama stayed with the company for the six years contracted. The estimate amounted to $4.5 million.

The parties in this case gave widely varying testimonies as to how this costly conflict got started and what each party knew about the other at the time the original contract was made. The varied assertions are a lawyer's delight—or, more accurately, several lawyers' delights.

Here is part of what former manager Larry McBride said:

> At the time I executed the exclusive agency agreement between International House of Talent, Inc., and Alabama, on behalf of Alabama, I had personal knowledge that International House of Talent, Inc., was in fact a corporation, and I intended for Alabama to enter into said agreement with the corporation. [In other words, McBride directly refuted Alabama's argument that it thought it was signing a contract with Dale Morris only.]
>
> One of the major reasons in signing Alabama to International House of Talent, Inc., was my understanding that Billy "Crash"

Craddock was affiliated with that agency, and Alabama would be able to make live personal appearances with him.

Here's how Randy Owen saw the whole thing:

> On May 22, 1980, McBride executed on behalf of Alabama an exclusive agency agreement *with Dale Morris* [emphasis added] doing business as International House of Talent, employing Mr. Morris's personal services to negotiate, secure, and execute on the group's behalf contracts for Alabama's concert performances throughout the country.
>
> Around the time this contract was executed, McBride informed us that he had employed Dale Morris to be our booking agent. Neither McBride nor anyone else discussed with the group or even mentioned any corporation or other entity named "International House of Talent" or any relationship of any nature between Dale Morris and Billy "Crash" Craddock. . . . It was our firm conviction then, and remains as such now, that we would never approve of any booking arrangement whereby another artist would be involved in securing concert appearances on our behalf because of what we consider a conflict of interest.

It was only after the fact of signing, Owen contended, that anyone in the Alabama group knew about Craddock's co-ownership of IHT:

> We never discussed with McBride or any other person the possibility of Alabama appearing at concerts with Craddock. The first time we became aware that we were booked with Craddock was at the concert performed on November 28, 1980, at Hickory, North Carolina, at which we "opened" for Craddock. The first time we became aware that Craddock shared ownership of the agency with Dale Morris was at the next concert on November 29, 1980, in Columbia, South Carolina. At that time, Craddock visited us in our dressing room and informed us that he owned a part of the agency. However, Craddock never discussed the extent of his interest in the agency, and we assumed that the agency was owned substantially by Mr. Morris.

Alabama's packaging with Craddock was a disappointment, according to Owen:

> Alabama was extremely displeased with these two concerts at which we "opened" for Craddock. We found that Craddock's style of performing, and the audiences to which that style appealed, conflicted severely with our goals and desires as a performing group and, therefore, in our opinion, continued association with him was not in the best interests of the group. Therefore, after completing these two concerts with Craddock, we informed Dale Morris and Barbara Hardin, his assistant, that for the above-stated reasons, Alabama would not perform on the same show with Craddock in the future, and since that time we have not done so.

In explaining the band's organization, Owen told the court that "although no member of the group is actually designated as the 'lead' or 'managing member,' at all times relevant [here], I was, in essence, the administrative head of the group, and third parties' contacts with Alabama were usually made through me."

Dale Morris, Craddock's one-time friend and manager—clearly the man in the middle of this tempest—recalls the events involved in the case this way:

> Sometime in January or February of 1980, Mr. Harold Shedd came to me to discuss the possibility of my booking a new, unknown group of recording artists called Alabama. I had known Mr. Shedd both socially and professionally for 10 or 12 years prior to this meeting, and we were

W. Craig Angle

In the years before he became Alabama's manager, Dale Morris (left) handled the career of country music star Billy "Crash" Craddock (right). Shown with the two one-time friends here is Ron Chancey, now producer for the Oak Ridge Boys. Morris and Chancey established the Cartwheel Records label on which Craddock had his first hit.

friends with each other. No one else attended that initial meeting. Because Mr. Shedd had brought the group to me and because, after listening to a recording of the group, I, too, thought they had potential, I told Mr. Shedd that I would be interested in taking a chance on the group. Soon after our first meeting, Mr. Shedd brought Mr. Lowery [Larry] McBride to see me. Mr. McBride was introduced to me as Alabama's manager. Prior to this occasion, I had never met or heard of Mr. McBride before.

In Morris's recollection, this first meeting with McBride centered on Alabama's booking needs and not on Morris's connection with IHT:

> Throughout the meeting, Mr. McBride emphasized to me that he had come to me on Harold Shedd's recommendation because he knew no one in the talent agency business and knew nothing about providing booking services. I explained the terms under which I would agree to book the group and Mr. McBride accepted those terms. At no time during our meeting did we discuss or even mention International House of Talent, Inc., or Crash Craddock.

This clearly contradicted McBride's testimony that the Craddock connection was a main cause for signing.

Alabama was not an immediate booking bonanza, as Morris recalls it:

> When we first started, we could not get as much as $750 per date for the group. I continued to operate under the terms of our [Morris's and McBride's] oral agreement for approximately two-and-a-half to three months before entering into a written exclusive agency agreement with Alabama. I had no written contracts with any of the

Melodie Gimple

Alabama poses with Larry McBride (second row, second from left). Harold Shedd (second row, second from right) and various RCA Records personnel.

> acts I booked, but it became necessary in this case because I found that Mr. McBride was frequently trying to make commitments for the group which were beginning to conflict with the personal appearance dates I was arranging.

Then the plot thickened, Morris said, when McBride asked him for some business assistance:

> In May, when Mr. McBride came to me seeking my assistance in obtaining credit, I insisted on his entering into a written exclusive agency agreement with me on behalf of the group Alabama. I had the contract drawn between Alabama and myself doing business as International House of Talent and not between Alabama and International House of Talent, Inc., largely because of Mr. McBride's insistence that I be personally responsible for the group and that Billy "Crash" Craddock, another recording artist and 50 percent owner of the agency, not be involved in any decisions concerning Alabama's personal appearances. The exclusive agency contract [dated May 22, 1980], simply memorialized the terms under which I and Alabama had been operating previously.

Morris testified that McBride's concerns about the Alabama-IHT agreement were quite restricted:

> All Mr. McBride ever wanted to know from me was how many dates I had obtained for Alabama and how much money I was able to charge for those dates. I continued to book [Alabama] under the [May 22, 1980] contract until shortly after the date [May 28, 1981] upon which I was

Melodie Gimple

Randy demonstrates his youth appeal.

removed without cause as an officer of International House of Talent, Inc. I then left International House of Talent, Inc., and opened my own talent agency, Dale Morris & Associates, Inc. Alabama desired that I continue to serve as their talent agent and I have done so. Since leaving, I have not participated in any way in any of the business or corporate affairs of International House of Talent, Inc. Mr. McBride continued to serve as Alabama's manager until approximately March of 1981 when he began serving a sentence in federal prison for acts unconnected with Alabama, myself, or our contract. Since that time, I have also functioned as Alabama's exclusive personal manager.

Harold Shedd, who coproduces Alabama's records, told the court during the early breach of contract hearings how he had helped bring Morris and Alabama together:

Approximately three years ago [this statement was made in October, 1982] I was doing some independent production for Mr. Lowery McBride and a small label called MDJ Records. I was invited to a showcase sponsored by MDJ Records and when I attended, I first heard the group Alabama. Shortly thereafter, Mr. McBride brought the members of the group Alabama into my studio to see whether I would be interested in working with them. The group and I were able to work together well, and the relationship grew, and I have been associated with them ever since. I have known Dale Morris for approximately 11 or 12 years. I first met him when he was with Cartwheel Records. He helped me with an act I was working with, and we have remained friends.

By Shedd's account, it was Morris's character and not just his connections that led to the first meeting about Alabama:

> I trusted Dale, and I knew he was running a booking agency. In January or February 1980, I went to see him to see if he would be interested in booking Alabama. I alone initiated this meeting because of our long friendship and my trust in him. No one else attended the meeting. At that time, I did not know who Dale was booking nor did I have any knowledge of or about the agency's form of business organization. I later learned that Dale was a part owner of a corporation called International House of Talent, but when I went to see Dale about Alabama, I had never heard of the corporation.

Shedd may, indeed, have been unaware of IHT's existence, but as far back as 1978, *Billboard's Country Music Sourcebook* carried a half-page ad for the company in which Craddock was spotlighted. Morris's name was not mentioned in the ad, however.

Shedd continued:

> At our meeting, Dale expressed interest in Alabama and asked me to bring the group's manager by to talk with him. I knew that Mr. McBride was Alabama's manager, but did not know him other than through the independent production I had done for him. I then arranged for Mr. McBride and myself to meet with Dale Morris. At the meeting, we discussed Dale's booking Alabama, the services he would render, and the terms and conditions for these services. Throughout this discussion, there was no mention of International House of Talent, Inc., or any other corporation or entity. The only subject discussed was whether Dale would be interested in booking Alabama and under what terms. Likewise, there was no mention of Billy "Crash" Craddock, whom I later learned was a part owner of International House of Talent, Inc.

In the end, the court agreed that Alabama had, indeed, breached its contract with IHT and awarded the agency $1,798,825.18 for commissions lost as a result of the breach. Alabama has been unsuccessful (as of late 1984) in its appeal of this decision and, in addition to the almost $2 million it has to pay IHT, has incurred large legal expenses.

Jim Rawlings

CHAPTER 6

ANOTHER ONE FOR THE BOOKS

Was the mighty Alabama finally starting to slip? At the 1983 Country Music Association Awards Show, the frisky quartet from Fort Payne had galloped onto the Grand Ole Opry stage three times to pick up the most publicized and highly regarded prizes in country music. First, Alabama's *The Closer You Get* had been named Album of the Year; then the four were cited as Vocal Group of the Year; and, to cap it all, they trotted off with the biggest prize of them all: Entertainer of the Year. It was their second straight year to win this award, and in so doing they had tied Barbara Mandrell's record. She had taken the top trophy in 1980 and '81.

But in 1984, Alabama was doing a lot of sitting in the audience and watching other stars accept the awards *they* had been nominated for. The Statlers, one of the wittiest and most consistently popular acts in the business, took the Vocal Group prize, a victory that must have seemed especially sweet to them, since they had won it every single year from 1972 through 1980, only to lose it the next two years to the boys from Alabama. Next, Anne Murray's *A Little Good News* album rolled over Alabama's *Roll On* to earn Album of the Year honors. Even their precious Instrumental Group of the Year award, which they had run away with in 1981 and '82, left the stage this year with the Ricky Skaggs Band. It was shaping up to be a bad night.

These losses were particularly unsettling coming as they did during a year in which everything else seemed so on target. Alabama had released its *Roll On* album in January and simultaneously announced that the R. J. Reynolds Tobacco Company would be sponsoring the group in a 120-city "Salem Spirit" concert tour. Within the next few months, Alabama had racked up

Alabama sings on the Grand Ole Opry stage with country music legend Roy Acuff.

two more number 1 singles in *Billboard*: "Roll On" in March and "When We Make Love" in June. And tonight, October 8, their third single from the album, "If You're Gonna Play in Texas (You Gotta Have a Fiddle in the Band)," was already in the top five and surely destined to go number 1 within a matter of weeks. This was also the year that Alabama's record label, RCA, announced that the group had sold more than 14 million albums. So there was some consolation in the knowledge that this was one of the few bad nights in an otherwise banner year.

Meanwhile, the awards show was unfolding at an unusually brisk pace. The affable Kenny Rogers was hosting the show, glancing nonchalantly at the giant cue cards being held up to him and rambling on with the ease and informality of one who has spent most of his life talking to large crowds. A thin and peppy Dolly Parton had pranced out to kick off the program with "Tennessee Homesick Blues" and then retreated for the remainder of the evening. A couple of hours earlier, she and Rogers had held a press conference in the nearby Opryland Hotel to announce their upcoming Christmas album and television special.

Besides fellow superstars and label-mates Parton and Rogers, Alabama could look around them and see the other big names who had been lured to Nashville for this most glittering, prize-giving orgy of them all. Nearby sat Willie Nelson and Kris Kristofferson. They were in town to premiere their new movie, *Songwriter*, and had stayed on to perform one of the numbers from the sound track. And over there were the Oak Ridge Boys, still beaming from their appearance on stage with the venerable Ray Charles in a number designed to spotlight his *Friendship* album. Ricky Skaggs, Janie Fricke, and B. J. Thomas had been up there with the Oaks and Charles, too.

ANOTHER ONE FOR THE BOOKS

Vernell Hackett

Alabama with Tony Seals, third from left, and Mentor Williams, writers of "When We Make Love."

Vernell Hackett

Randy Owen poses with (from left) Mentor Williams; Larry Henley, co-writer of "Wind Beneath My Wings;" Maggie Cavender, executive director of the Nashville Songwriters Association; and Kenny O'Dell, writer of "Mama He's Crazy."

Vernell Hackett

On this particular evening, Alabama hadn't spent all its time in the audience. One of the biggest production numbers had featured "If You're Gonna Play in Texas." It had started out simply enough with just Alabama playing. But cluster by cluster, more and more fiddlers joined them onstage until, at the last note, there must have been 40 or so fiddlers, young and old, male and female, sawing away as the crowd down front clapped enthusiastically in rhythm.

Then it was back into the audience for Alabama to watch other artists win and other stars perform. The redirected rock band Exile, already shaping up as rivals to Alabama, made its CMA Awards Show debut with the ingratiating "Give Me One More Chance." Lee Greenwood, who would again be crowned Male Vocalist of the Year, spoke a short tribute to his singing partner, Barbara Mandrell, who was still recovering from a near-fatal car wreck. Lee sang his version of their first duet record, "To Me." Then Reba McEntire gave a tearful acceptance speech upon being picked Female Vocalist of the Year, dedicating her award to "me and my mama."

As the awards show neared its end, a regal Loretta Lynn swept up to the microphone and, without referring to her own recent loss of a son, spoke eloquently about the loss of her friend and mentor, Ernest Tubb. Then she sang his trademark, "Walkin' the Floor over You," while the audience stood in recognition of Tubb's great influence on country music and Lynn's great courage in the face of her latest adversity.

Because it means the most in both publicity and industry esteem, the Entertainer of the Year award is the last one given. Adding to this contrived suspense this year was the fact that the live show was running a few minutes over. But finally the names of the nominees for the award were read: Alabama, Lee Greenwood, Barbara Mandrell, Ronnie Milsap, and the Oak Ridge Boys.

Even among the industry's insiders, the bets were evenly spread, with no one acknowledged as a front-runner. Greenwood, although a relative newcomer, had a lot going for him. He had won the Male Vocalist award last year as well as this year. In addition, he had teamed with the popular Mandrell and released a surprisingly well-received swatch of chauvinism called "God Bless the U.S.A." Besides, he had demonstrated himself to be an all-around entertainer, whether playing his expert sax or crooning intimate encouragement to middle-age hearts. He was certifiably hot and a real contender.

Mandrell, although her record prominence was sagging, was now into making television movies. Her variously titled effort ("Coal Fire," "Burning Rage," etc.) with Tom Wopat had been getting a lot of publicity. And, as mentioned, just before the movie aired, she and her children had been involved in a terrible accident. These factors, combined with the force of her two previous wins, certainly made her a sentimental favorite.

Milsap also had points going for him. He was making a big push in the pop direction, and his splashy and star-studded music video on "She Loves My Car" was even being shown on the usually country-free MTV. No charity case here.

The Oaks had had a good year, too. Their records were going number 1 with clocklike regularity. Each of the Oaks was developing greater recognition among country audiences, especially the sartorially flamboyant (if otherwise low-key) Bill Golden. And stung by the fact that they were consistently taking a backseat to Alabama in concert revenues, the Oaks had spent hundreds of thousands of dollars to perk up their stage shows. Moreover, they had one of the most imaginative publicity mechanisms in the business.

Alabama was no slouch, though, for the reasons already cited. They had won more than their share of other industry honors throughout 1984 and were far and away the biggest concert draw and record sellers.

In those few seconds between the tearing of the envelope flap and the proclamation of the name inside, the nerves of the nominees tear, also. "What to say if I win? How to act if I lose?"

"The winner of the Entertainer of the Year award is . . . Alabama!"

Instantly relieved, confidence and good spirits miraculously restored—Randy Owen, Teddy Gentry, Jeff Cook, and Mark Herndon leaped to their feet, trampled on other feet as they edged out of their row and into the aisle, and romped and jumped toward the stage. By now the trip up was old-hat—but it meant absolutely everything right now. For the first time in the history of the Country Music Association, an act had been named Entertainer of the Year three times in a row. It was another one for the books.

72

Melodie Gimple

CHAPTER 7

THE FUTURE OF ALABAMA

Can Alabama survive? As a solid money-making act, of course it can. But at its present level of acceptance, almost certainly not. Randy Owen, himself, said it best: "History's not going to change for us."

The Statler Brothers, whose professional life Alabama has followed so closely, had their first hit in 1966, with "Flowers on the Wall," and they've been going strong ever since, in spite of the fact that their sound is incredibly old-fashioned. They have kept their high rank in country music by developing the superb songwriting talents within their own ranks; handling their own publishing; finding a congenial record label and sticking with it without demanding it perform marketing miracles; finding and retaining a producer who understands their strengths; keeping personnel changes within the quartet to a minimum (only one switch since the group started, and that because of illness, not discontent); targeting and playing to an audience of early-middle-agers and up (the kind not given to sudden switches of musical interest); and by locating their principal place of doing business well away from Nashville's pointless distractions.

The Oak Ridge Boys have done essentially the same thing—except for seeking a wider audience and recording more material written outside their organization. The Oaks have been consistently hot since 1977.

Larry Gatlin and the Gatlin Brothers Band is yet another example of an act that has stayed profitably intact by following the formula of tight inside control—although Larry Gatlin's flagging appeal as the trio's sole source of songs did seem to endanger the group's radio popularity briefly in the early '80s.

Concluded on page 77.

IN CONCERT

Alabama plays Nashville's Centennial Park.

Melodie Gimple

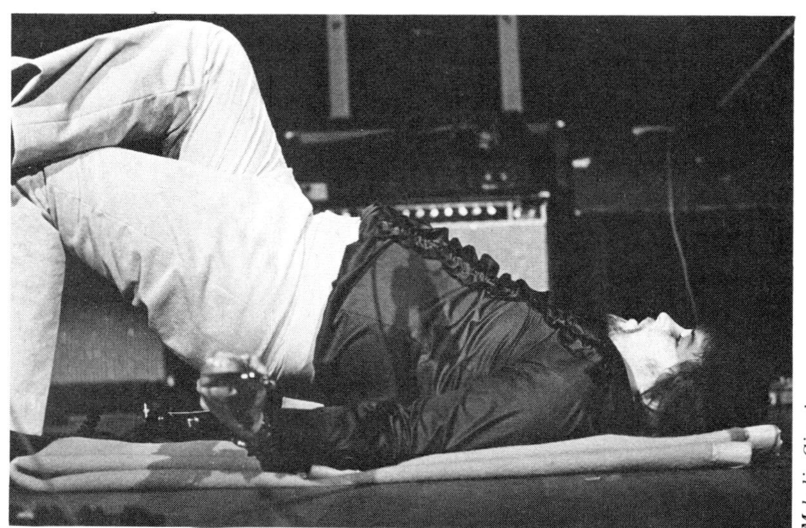

Melodie Gimple

Apparently bored by picking in an upright position, lead guitarist Jeff Cook lies down on the job.

Larry Dixon

All photos by Larry Dixon

Larry Dixon

Continued from page 73

None of the groups just cited, though, have a member who towers above the others with the across-the-board sex appeal that Randy Owen generates. Groups are more likely to stick together when record and ticket buyers can spread their attention and affection fairly equally among the different members.

Having weathered the storms this long, there is no reason to believe that Alabama will suddenly fall prey to that fatal internal dissension that has killed so many acts. The three principals have apparently come to terms with each other's personalities and are all sensible enough to appreciate their dependence on one another. Even with his less than equal share of the corporate pie, Herndon realizes he has stumbled into a dream job for one of his limited professional experience. So there are all these reasons to believe—and even to bet—that Alabama can stay afloat on many more miles of troubled waters.

Vernell Hackett

CHAPTER 8

THE ALABAMA EMPIRE

On the several walls of awards, tributes, and citations displayed at Alabama's fan club headquarters in Fort Payne, there is one small Texas-shaped plaque on which is inscribed all there is to be said about the business part of the music business. It reads:

Alabama
Majestic Theatre • Oct. 11, 1980 • 238 Tickets Sold
Randy's • April 17, 1981 • 1,040 Tickets Sold
Convention Center Arena • Sept. 28, 1981 • 5,240 Tickets Sold
Joe Freeman Coliseum • Sept. 3, 1981 • 7,267 Tickets Sold
Convention Center • Nov. 11, 1983 • "Sold Out"
Congratulations From The Staff Of Rainbow Ticketmaster
San Antonio, Texas, 1983

In the music business, you sell tickets and records or else you go back to your day job. It is all very brutally simple. Alabama had its seven-year tenure at the Bowery for no other reason than they were able to pack the Bowery night after night.

FOR WHAT THEY'RE WORTH

A list of the band's gross income from concerts which was filed as an exhibit in one of the suits brought against Alabama reveals that between May 13, 1981, and November 21 of the same year, Alabama grossed $829,088.73. Just a few months earlier they had been playing for tips.

And that was peanuts compared to what came later. In 1982, Alabama's gross concert income was $7,300,265.34 for 136 shows. During the first eight-and-a-half months of 1983, the band grossed $6,223,385.44 through its concerts. In April, 1983, alone, the gross concert revenue amounted to $1,218,817.44.

In one day, on which Alabama did two concerts at the same place, the gross was $201,452.20. Between May 13, 1981, and

Edward Morris

One of Alabama's tour buses. When it was performing as Wildcountry, the group travelled in a single van.

August 15, 1983, the concert grosses totalled $14,352,739.51.

In 1984, the R. J. Reynolds Tobacco Company agreed to sponsor Alabama's 120-date "Salem Spirit" tour. Not only did the tobacco company help underwrite the cost of the tour and, thus, relieve Alabama's costs, it also paid the group an undisclosed fee for the association of the company's name with the band's name.

As enormous as these sums are, concerts represent only a part of Alabama's earnings picture. There is also a huge income from record sales. According to the most recent RCA tally, the group had sold more than 14 million albums.

It is difficult to determine how much Alabama earns from its album sales, but one can make some educated guesses by referring to court documents. One reveals that when Alabama's one-time manager Larry McBride signed the group to RCA Records, his company's royalty share was 12 percent (apparently of the usual retail price of the albums). At that time, the document says, Alabama had a 5 percent royalty, presumably their part of McBride's percentage. This was still early in the band's career, back when they had sold only two million albums.

Two million albums at a suggested retail price of $8.98 each amounts to $17,960,000. Five percent of this figure is $898,000. Later, when the management contract with McBride was ended, one can be sure that Alabama had the economic muscle and the legal counsel to raise its percentage to something at least in the neighborhood of what McBride had been able to bargain for from RCA when the act was still relatively unproven. It would be idle speculation to guess what the act's current percentage is. But if one took a conservative guess of 10 percent and applied that to the number of albums sold, then one sees another gigantic source of revenue.

Besides its share as the recording artists from record sales, Alabama derives an additional royalty by being coproducers of its own albums. According to one Alabama-related court document, three percent of the suggested retail price of records sold is the usual and customary percentage paid jointly to the producers in the industry. On the first two RCA albums, Alabama shared production credits with Larry McBride and Harold Shedd. (Sonny Limbo also produced two of the ten songs on the first album.) On the next three albums, though, the production is split just between Alabama and Shedd.

Additionally, there is significant publishing income from songs the members write and/or have publishing rights to—income from the songs being performed on radio and television, in clubs, etc.; income from "mechanicals" (that is, from record and tape sales of their songs); and income from their songs being printed as sheet music and in books. A music accountant estimates that a "successful" songwriter in country music will earn $100,000 a year and up. The songwriters within Alabama are more than "successful" since they record their own songs and sell more records than any other country artist. Moreover, they own all or part of the publishing rights to these songs. So, again, the writing and publishing incomes are substantial.

And as everyone who has attended an Alabama concert or joined its fan club knows, the band sells all sorts of merchandise: albums, bandanas, belt buckles, fans, garters, hand towels, hat pins, highball glasses, key chains, knives, license plates, lighters, mugs, playing cards, songbooks, sunglasses, suspenders, and much more. Alabama's fan club newsletters in 1984 were listing approximately 90 separate items for sale. And these newsletter/catalogs were being sent to more than 200,000 fans.

It is impossible to make even an educated guess about the income from the sale of

Edward Morris

This is Alabama's home-away-from-home in Nashville. It is located on 19th Avenue, South.

Edward Morris

In this modest frame house, across 18th Avenue, South, from the Music Mill recording studio, Maggie Cavender administers Alabama's publishing company, Maypop Music. The building is also the headquarters of the Nashville Songwriters Association, International, of which Cavender is executive director.

Edward Morris

Alabama's manager Dale Morris's office building stands next door to the "Bama House" on Nashville's 19th Avenue, South.

Alabama merchandise. Some artists make as much selling merchandise at a concert as they do selling tickets.

Besides the buildings and other real estate Alabama owns or leases in common, Owen and Gentry each own cattle farms. Gentry and his wife also operate a kennel in Fort Payne. Jeff Cook has a recording studio and a clothing store in Augusta, Georgia. There are Alabama gift shops in Fort Payne, Nashville, and Myrtle Beach.

Because the band is so often in Nashville to record or do business with its manager, record label, or publishing companies, the four members have set up a home-away-from-home on 19th Avenue South, in the famous "Music Row" area. They call it "Bama House" or "The Compound."

The Bama House is located next door to manager Dale Morris's office and just a couple of doors down from their ad agency, MAF Advertising. A short walk around the corner takes Alabama to its publishing company, Maypop Music, which is itself directly across 18th Avenue South from Music Mill recording studio, where the group cuts its albums. And Music Mill is only a hundred or so steps away from Alabama's record label headquarters. It's all very close and very cozy—and a monumental I-told-you-so to the scoffers and non-believers of not too long ago.

Even in the fullness of success, then, circumstances have contrived to keep the members of Alabama close to and still dependent on each other, whether in their tiny hometown, their walled-in compound in Nashville, their sleek tour buses, or on the small, cluttered stages that serve as their launching platforms to even greater successes.

THE COST OF DOING BUSINESS

All income is not gravy, though. To begin with, Alabama has substantial road costs: leasing and paying the operating costs of a fleet of buses and trucks is a major expense. It will cost $500 a day or more to operate a single bus. Alabama has several buses, plus equipment and merchandise trucks. Add to this the cost of food and lodging for the band and road crew, the cost of security, insurance, staging, etc., and the bottom line gets whittled down a bit. Subtract also the booking agent's commission on shows. Of the $14 million concert gross cited earlier, almost $1.5 million went to the booking agency.

Depending on who you ask or what you read, the Alabama organization has 40 to 50 full-time employees, and they are said to be well paid and furnished with a substantial benefit package. If the average employee costs Alabama only $20,000 a year in salary and benefits—and many must earn far more than that—then this expenditure alone would amount to between $800,000 and $1 million annually.

Dennis Benefield

While Alabama gets artist and producer royalties from its record sales, it also has to pay (in the long run) for the production costs—studio rental for recording and mixing the master tapes, and the costs of hiring musicians and engineers.

To sell tons of merchandise, Alabama has to buy, transport, store, and ship tons of it. And it's expensive every step of the way. More than most acts, Alabama has kept its merchandise prices as low as possible. In fact, they are so concerned about this point that they once threatened to boycott auditoriums that insisted on cutting themselves in for a high percentage of merchandise sold on the premises. To have gone along with this, Alabama argued, would make it force the prices too high. The fans would be forced to absorb the extra cost, and Alabama wouldn't have that. While these concerns are admirable, they do have the effect of cutting down on the band's profit margin.

Alabama's is one of the few—if not the only—major fan club that charges the fan nothing to join and receive the periodic newsletters. While the cynical may say that this is just an effective way to set up a buying mechanism for the band's merchandise, the fact of the matter is that one can stay a member and not buy a penny's worth of memorabilia. And the club is costly to maintain. Besides the costs of composing and printing the newsletters, it is quite costly to mail them. Alabama's fan club postage for the summer, 1984, quarter alone was $22,250.36.

So vast is the band's concert operation that its manager Dale Morris told *Music City News*: "When you take time off it really costs you with an operation like we've got." Morris illustrated his point by noting that when the band took off two weeks in July, 1983, it cost the organization "about $450,000."

CHARITABLE WORK

If Alabama's great earnings have attracted lawsuits and business headaches, they have also enabled the group to do a lot of good for others besides themselves. It is common for performers to make contributions to charity. From a strictly cynical point of view, such contributions are both good publicity and good tax savers. But Alabama has put a lot of thought into the long list of charities to which it contributes.

In 1982, Alabama held its first "June Jam" in Fort Payne as a way of earning money to benefit all of DeKalb County. The event was so wildly successful that the group has held similar outdoor music festivals in Fort Payne every summer since. Not only are the total proceeds from ticket sales donated to the community, so is the income from all the concession and souvenir stands. Hardly an institution or organization in the Fort Payne area goes untouched by this benefit.

The list of beneficiaries of the 1983 June

Edward Morris

Two American institutions: Alabama and McDonald's. The sign marks the Alabama Fan Club complex in Fort Payne.

Jam—which raised $375,000—is four crowded pages long and illustrates the range of Alabama's concerns:

• The DeKalb County Library Board got a grant of $23,000 to complete its part of a matching-fund program that ultimately brought it a total of $150,000.

• Jeff Cook's old grade school—where he gave perhaps his first public performance when he was six years old—got $1,000 for its Reading Is Fundamental program, another matching-fund setup with a three-to-one payoff.

• Historically minded Alabama saw to it that some of its Jam money went toward the restoration of the old Fort Payne Depot, $1,000; for Landmarks of DeKalb County to install historical markers, $2,000; and for repairs and maintenance of a monument at the Chickamauga Battle Grounds, $1,425.

• In its concern for the elderly, Alabama gave the Retired Senior Volunteer Program $10,540; the Care Assurance Programs for the Aging and Homebound, $1,250; and the Mayor's Advisory Council for the Elderly in Geraldine, Alabama, $5,000.

• Special Olympics got $2,000; the Regional Alcoholism Council, $1,000; the Fort Payne Boxing League, $2,000; the DeKalb County Health Department, $5,000 (to start a dental clinic); the Diabetes Association, $1,200; the Association for Retarded Children, $5,000; the DeSoToe Square Dance Club, $1,000; the Alabama Council of the Blind, $1,000; the National Kidney Foundation, $1,000; the Moon Lake Elementary School gym construction fund, $10,000; and the Children's Hospital in Birmingham, $5,000.

• Alabama gave twenty-one area volunteer fire departments $2,000 each, and ten school bands a total of $25,000.

There were literally dozens of other similarly needy and grateful recipients on the 1983 list and the 1984 funds were distributed with equal care and precision.

THEIR HOME IN ALABAMA

It is not a "Hee Haw" joke or a citified reporter's wisecrack. Fort Payne really does refer to itself as "The Sock Capital of the World." In fact, in one recent Chamber of Commerce brochure, the sock slogan had top billing over that of Fort Payne's favorite sons, Alabama.

Well, neither the sock nor the strip designation does the town justice. Fort Payne is a clean, apparently bustling community of about 14,000, comfortably squeezed in between Lookout Mountain on the east and Sand Mountain on the west. The town is home to factories (garbage truck bodies, structural steel, electric transformers, playground equipment) and farms (soybeans, potatoes, poultry, and livestock). Except for being Baptist dry, Fort Payne could be any small town, north or south of the Mason-Dixon line.

Fort Payne takes its name from a man who participated in one of America's more shameful chapters in history—the driving of the Cherokees from their tribal territo-

Edward Morris

Alabama's fan club headquarters and merchandise warehouse in Fort Payne.

ries in the east onto the genocidal "Trail of Tears" death march to the west. The drive started in Chattanooga, Tennessee, about 50 miles northeast of where Fort Payne now stands, in 1838. That same year, U.S. Army Captain John Payne established a fort along Big Wills Creek in northeast Alabama to serve as a base for his troops in their part of the Cherokee banishment. Ironically, the creek itself had been named in honor of the Cherokee chief, Big Wills. Around this military base grew the town of Fort Payne, which in 1876 was declared the seat of DeKalb County.

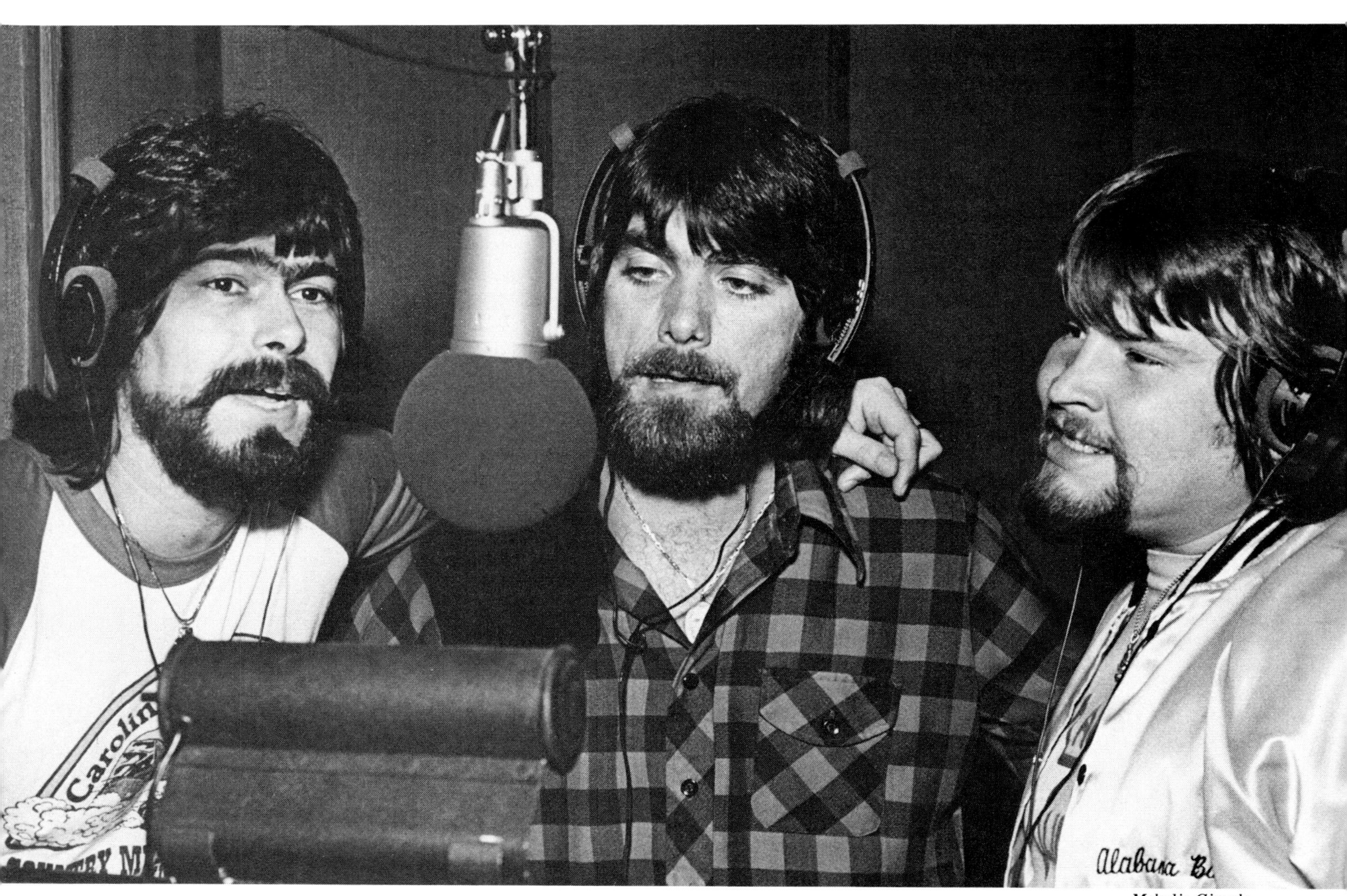

Melodie Gimple

CHAPTER

9

THE BOYS IN THE STUDIO

Old-time country music artists generally had little patience with or interest in the recording studio. In its infancy, the recording process was so painstaking and technically limited that the performers could expect that only a minimum of their overall artistry would shine through. But with the invention of multitrack recording, by which songs could be recorded in layers (each of which could be done at separate times and edited separately), the studio became a place not only for the recording of art but also for the creation of it.

The rock 'n' roll generation grew up just as the techniques of recording were making the most rapid advances. And, as a part of that generation, Alabama has the same outlook toward recording that any modern rock band would have. Unlike their musical ancestor, Roy Acuff, whose impatience with recording earned him the name of "One-Take Ake," Alabama plans and polishes each song for an album in an effort to make the recorded performance as lively as the stage one. That goal translates into long, expensive, and exhaustive hours in the studio.

Except for a few random tracks, all of the songs on Alabama's RCA albums have been recorded at producer Harold Shedd's Music Mill studios, situated on Roy Acuff Place and 18th Avenue South, only a few blocks from the old studio. Because of its log cabin exterior, the new studio is sometimes referred to as "Fort Shedd."

Alabama and Shedd constantly screen songs to get the cream for the group's once-a-year album projects, and they block off sizable sections of the year to record the album meticulously. There's nothing quick or last-minute about this process—which is understandable considering the millions of dollars of recording and publishing income

Edward Morris

The Music Mill—the recording studio in which Alabama cuts its albums. The studio is located on Roy Acuff Place in Nashville, across the street from Alabama's publishing company and around the corner from the RCA Records headquarters (below).

Alabama, producer Harold Shedd and RCA's Joe Galante (behind lamp) listen to the playback at the old Music Mill studio.

involved. Shedd, who has overseen records for Connie Francis, Mel Tillis, Glen Campbell, and Reba McEntire, among others, has been Alabama's coproducer since its MDJ Records days.

A tall, thin, and remarkably friendly man, Shedd has been working as a producer in Nashville for more than a dozen years. His reputation in this field, according to *Billboard*'s Kip Kirby, rests on his "crisp, punchy arrangements, rather than [on] lavish productions or typical 'Nashville-sounding' instrumentation and backgrounds."

About his work with Alabama, Shedd told a reporter for *Music Row* magazine, "We've tried to do different types of music that still say some of the same things. These guys are real serious about their music, so we're always interested in a different kind of song. A 'Mountain Music' is different from a 'Feels So Right,' yet the same people liked both songs. So, obviously, you can take different approaches as long as you don't get too far away from the things you do best. We spend a lot of time discussing even the sequence in which the songs are going to appear on the album."

Randy Owen has often stated that the band's prime concern in selecting a song to record is, "Will it work on stage?" Alabama's agonizingly long apprenticeship at the Bowery has made the band members acutely aware of the need to please the crowd, right from the moment the group hits the stage.

To save time and still get the best musical sound possible, Alabama (like most other country acts) relies almost entirely on the services of a corps of Nashville's most versatile studio musicians. (Whether the omission is intentional isn't clear, but none of the backup musicians for the 1980 New Faces show have ever played on an Alabama album.)

One musician who has worked with Alabama on all its RCA albums (and even some

Alabama with the executives from the Nashville division of RCA Records. Joe Galante, third from left, heads the division. Jerry Bradley, third from right, was top man of the division when RCA signed Alabama.

earlier projects) is keyboard virtuoso Willie Rainsford. Here he describes what it's like to record with Alabama:

"Basically, it's a very loose situation where everybody contributes. We usually book three sessions a day—at ten, two, and six [o'clock]. It's a very relaxed atmosphere. We go in and get the [right] drum sound and get the mikes set up. Usually the guys are upstairs [in the Music Mill] with Harold, going over the songs they want to do for that session. We go for one song—however long it takes. We play it until we get the arrangement down to where it feels good—where it's got that energy. And we'll play it over and over again. Randy likes to get the basic vocal down on it with piano, bass, drums, two rhythm guitars, and lead."

Relaxed though the scene may be, the work is hard, Rainsford stresses: "When I get through working, it's been very draining. . . . They try to get it down the way they'd do it on stage. Sometimes they'll say, 'We can't do it this way, because Jeff will be doing this, and he won't have time to get off his guitar and get into the fiddle part.' They take that all into consideration when they're putting [a song] together."

Even when the studio clock is running, according to Rainsford, the emphasis is on doing it right rather than getting it done. Always, there is a willingness to take the time and spend the money to get the satisfactory sound: "We had this one song we worked on all day long. We'd take it apart, because someone would say, 'It don't feel right.' That's another thing they like—trying a song different ways with different instrumentation. 'Lady Down on Love' we tried a bunch of different ways, and it ended up with Randy just playing the guitar and singing. I went in later and played the electric piano for the beginning of it."

Of Shedd, Rainsford observes, "Harold has a good ear for a song. To me, that's where it begins. What feels right—that's the key." The variety of session players helps Alabama achieve its distinctive sound, Rainsford believes: "We have some real country guys, some who play rhythm and blues, and some young guys who cut up and play things differently." The prevailing attitude in the studio, he says, is "Try it, you might like it."

Musicians never hear the finished product until the album is out, Rainsford admits. "On 'If You're Gonna Play in Texas,' there was a part—I think it's on the album—where the piano plays a little of 'The Eyes of Texas Are upon You' on the intro. But on the single, they took that off. I think it was because of the time."

Not only has Rainsford been able to watch the members of Alabama mature as performers, he's been able to witness the way they've adjusted to greater and greater celebrity. He thinks they've handled stardom very well. "They don't act like, 'Hey, I'm here. The world can start now.' Every year, they take us down to Fort Payne for the Christmas party, and they try to recognize everybody. That means a lot. That means more a lot of times than money—to be needed."

Rainsford reports that even amid the tedium of studio work, Alabama has been able to keep its perspective about what is most important: "On the last session I was in, Randy said, 'Boys, we sure are lucky to be in here and doing what we love to do.' That really says it all."

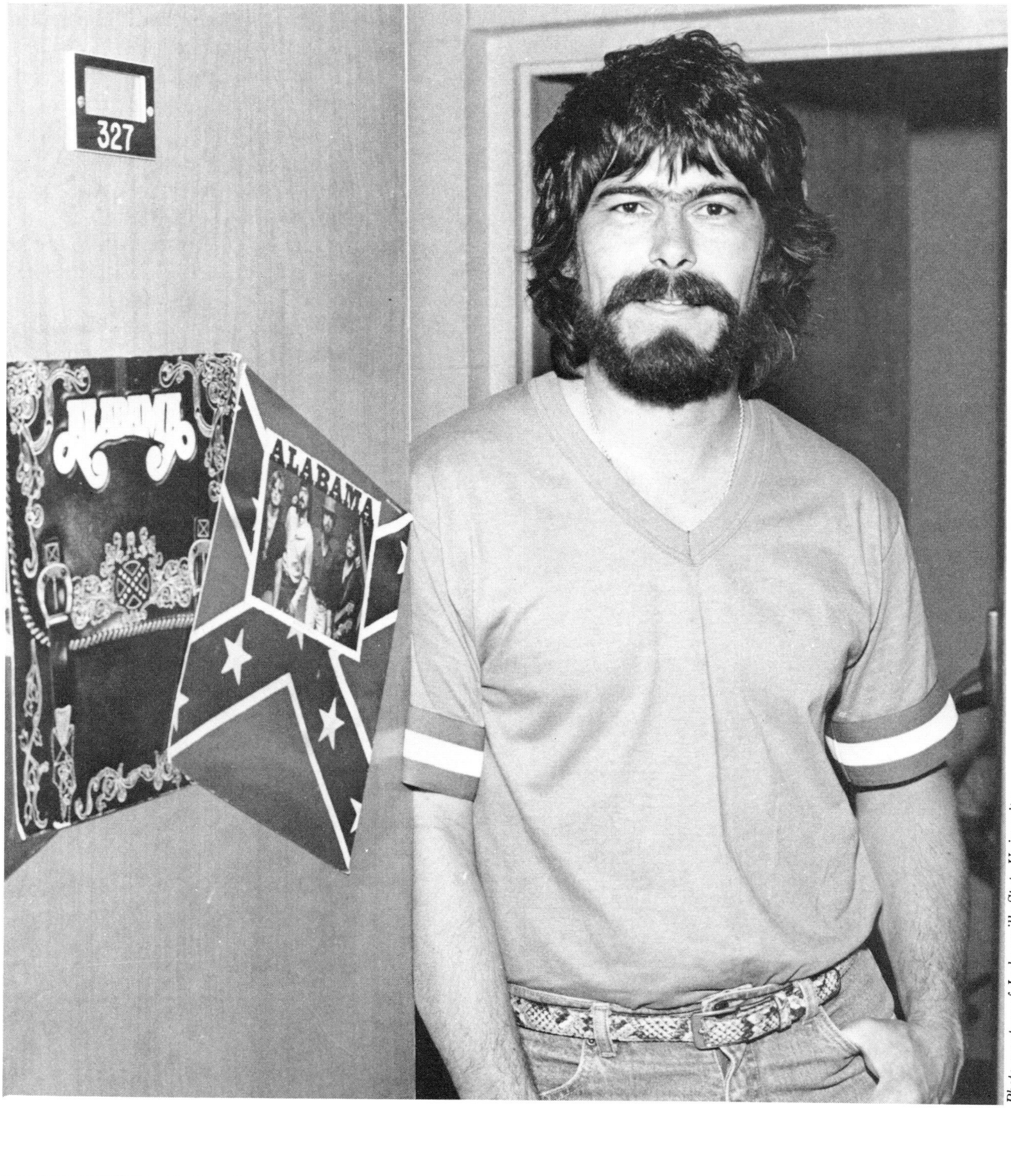

Photo courtesy of Jacksonville State University

CHAPTER 10

AN ALABAMA ALMANAC

1838

- Colonel John Payne builds a fort along Big Wills Creek in northern Alabama to serve as a base for his removal of the last of the Cherokee Indians in the region. From this base grows the town of Fort Payne.

1949

- August 27—Jeffrey Alan Cook born in Fort Payne.
- December 13—Randy Yeuell Owen born in Fort Payne.

1952

- January 22—Teddy Wayne Gentry born in Fort Payne.

1955

- May 11—Mark Joel Herndon born in Springfield, Massachusetts.

1963

- August 30—Jeff Cook takes DJ job at WFPA, Fort Payne.

1967

- Jeff Cook graduates from high school.

1969

- Randy Owen graduates from high school; enters Northeast State Junior College near Rainsville.
- Young Country, a band that includes Randy, Jeff, and Teddy, is formed.

Two generations of Alabama greats. At center is Grand Ole Opry member Charlie Louvin, who, with his brother, Ira, established one of the most influential groups in country music history. The Louvin Brothers came from Henagar, Alabama, just a few miles away from Fort Payne.

1970

- Teddy Gentry graduates from high school.
- July 20—Jeff Cook awarded a diploma in electronics from Alabama Technical College, Gadsden.

1972

- Spring—The band Wildcountry forms with Cook as lead guitarist; Owen, lead vocalist and rhythm guitarist; Gentry, bassist; and Bennett Vartanian, drummer.
- July 3—Wildcountry makes its first professional appearance, opening for, and backing, Gordon Terry at Canyonland Park near Fort Payne.

1973

- March 5—Wildcountry appears for the first time at the Bowery club in Myrtle Beach, South Carolina.
- Spring—Randy Owen graduates from Jacksonville (AL) State University with a BA in English and an overall "B" average.
- October—Wildcountry incorporates; es-

During a visit to **Billboard** *magazine, Alabama and publicist Greg Fowler (left) clown with receptionist Renee Beams.*

tablishes Maypop Music as its publishing company.

- Fall—Wildcountry records its first custom album.

1974

- Band goes to Nashville to look for a recording deal.
- T. Howard Hamilton, later a short-term manager for Alabama, is convicted in Texas of conspiring to defraud a savings and loan association.

1975

- Wildcountry records the single "Sweet Country Woman"/"Try Me."
- Wildcountry records an album: *Wildcountry.*
- Wildcountry records demonstration tapes (demos) that will later be released (illegally, a court decides) as *Alabama: Pride of Dixie* and *Alabama: Wild Country.*

1976

- February—Bennett Vartanian leaves Wildcountry and is replaced as drummer by Jackie Owen, a cousin to Randy and Teddy.
- Jackie Owen quits band because of illness and is replaced by Rick Scott.
- Mark Herndon, who will join Alabama as drummer in 1979, drops out of Francis Marion College, Florence, South Carolina.

1977

- Band changes name from Wildcountry to Alabama.
- July 23—Alabama's "I Wanna Be with You Tonight," on GRT Record, debuts on Billboard's Hot Country Singles chart and eventually peaks at number 77.

1978

- October—Larry McBride, later Alabama's manager and record label head, is convicted in North Carolina of conspiracy and wire fraud.

1979

- Alabama records "I Wanna Come Over" on Limbo International Records from which it is later picked up and re-released by Larry McBride's MDJ label.
- Rick Scott leaves the band.
- March 9—Billy "Crash" Craddock and Dale Morris incorporate International House of Talent, Inc., a booking agency, with each owning 50 percent of the stock.
- April 1—Mark Herndon's first official day as Alabama's drummer.

1980

- January—"My Home's in Alabama"/"Why Lady Why" released on MDJ label.
- March 15—Alabama performs on the New Faces show at the Country Radio Seminar in Nashville.
- March 28—Alabama signs an exclusive recording agreement with MDJ Records.
- Alabama signs management contract with Larry McBride.
- April 11—McBride signs Alabama to RCA Records.
- May 16—RCA releases "Tennessee River"/"Can't Forget about You."
- May—RCA releases the album *My Home's in Alabama.*
- May 22—McBride signs Alabama to an exclusive three-year booking agreement with International House of Talent that gives the agency the option to renew for an additional three years.
- August 16—"Tennessee River" goes to number 1 in *Billboard*'s country charts—Alabama's first number 1.
- September 9—RCA releases "Why Lady Why"/"I Wanna Come Over."
- November 28/29—Alabama opens concerts for Billy "Crash" Craddock in Hickory, NC, and Columbia, SC. In court documents later, Alabama says it didn't approve of the kind of show Craddock was doing nor of the audience he appealed to and that this was the first time it learned of his connection to International House of Talent.
- December 13—"Why Lady Why" goes number 1.
- December 23—McBride gives his power of attorney to T. Howard Hamil-

Paul Natkin/Photo Reserve

ton, who subsequently steps in as the group's manager.

1981

- January—Alabama opens its first fan club at 813 Sanders Avenue, Fort Payne.
- January 23—"Old Flame"/"I'm Stoned" released.
- February—The album *Feels So Right* released.
- February 26—Craddock and Morris meet in Greensboro, NC, to discuss their personal management agreement.
- March 12—Morris becomes Alabama's manager by two-to-one vote.
- April 18—"Old Flame" goes number 1.
- April 30—The Academy of Country Music votes Alabama Vocal Group of the Year.
- May 1—"Feels So Right"/"See the Embers, Feel the Flame" released.
- May 27—The album *Feels So Right* is certified "gold" (sale of 500,000 copies) by the Recording Industry Association of America (RIAA).
- May 28—Directors of the International House of Talent remove Dale Morris from his corporate office.
- June 10—Morris forms Dale Morris & Associates with Alabama as its client.
- July 14—The album *My Home's in Alabama* is certified "gold."
- July 18—"Feels So Right" goes number 1.
- August—Fan club moves to 208 Gault Avenue, Fort Payne.
- September 4—"Love in the First Degree"/"Ride the Train" released.
- September 15—The album *Feels So Right* certifed "platinum" (sale of 1,000,000 copies).
- October 3—International House of

Vernell Hackett

Talent sues Alabama for the 10 percent commission amount the agency estimates it would have due if Alabama had stayed with the company for the six years originally contracted. IHT estimated its percentage as amounting to $4.5 million.

- October 12—Country Music Association names Alabama Instrumental Group and Vocal Group of the Year.
- November 25—Alabama sues to restrain RCA from distributing royalties from the sale of records to Dallas Banking & Trust for debts incurred by McBride.
- December 20—"Love in the First Degree" goes number 1.
- December 23—"Mountain Music"/ "Never Be One" released.

1982

- "Early" 1982—Fan club moves to 2207 Gault Avenue North, Fort Payne.
- February—The album *Mountain Music* released.
- March—Alabama granted injunction against the sale of the unauthorized album *Alabama: Pride of Dixie* and *Alabama: Wild Country*—made from demo tapes recorded in 1975.
- April 29—Academy of Country Music awards Alabama Entertainer of the Year, Vocal Group of the Year, and Album of the Year (for *Feels So Right*). The album *Mountain Music* certified platinum.
- May 1—"Mountain Music" goes number 1.
- May 6—"Take Me Down"/"Lovin' You Is Killin' Me" released.
- June 4—Alabama holds its first June Jam to raise funds for educational and charitable organizations in the Fort Payne area.
- June 30—The album *My Home's in Alabama* is certified platinum.
- July 24—"Take Me Down" goes number 1.
- McBride sues Alabama's producer Harold Shedd for money he alleged to be due him from their earlier partnership.
- August 19—"Close Enough to Perfect"/ "Fantasy" released.
- September—Fan club moves to a former car dealership building at 201 Glenn Avenue SW, Fort Payne.
- October 11—The Country Music Association names Alabama Entertainer, Vocal Group, and Instrumental Group of the Year. This is the first time that a group has earned Entertainer of the Year status.
- October 16—First recording session at Jeff Cook's Cook Sound Studios.
- October 30—"Close Enough to Perfect" goes number 1.
- October 31—Alabama makes its first Grand Ole Opry appearance.
- November 5—The single "Christmas in Dixie" released.

Paul Natkin/Photo Reserve

- This year, Mark Herndon earned his pilot's license.

1983

- January 15—"Christmas in Dixie" peaks at number 35, the first single with RCA not to go number 1.
- January 24—The single "Dixieland Delight" released.
- February 23—Alabama wins its first Grammy—Best Country Performance by a Duo or Group for "Mountain Music."
- March—The album *The Closer You Get* released.
- March—Chancery Court in Nashville rules that Alabama is in breach of contract with International House of Talent.
- April 16—"Dixieland Delight" goes number 1.
- April 20—The single "The Closer You Get" released.
- May 3—The album *The Closer You Get* is certified platinum.
- May 9—Alabama wins the Academy of Country Music's Vocal Group and Entertainer of the Year awards.
- June 11—Second June Jam held.

- June 14—Alabama receives appreciation plaque from the National PTA Convention in Albuquerque.
- July 16—"The Closer You Get" goes number 1.
- August 8—The single "Lady Down on Love" released.
- October 10—Alabama wins Country Music Association awards as Vocal Group and Entertainer of the Year and for Album of the Year (for *The Closer You Get*).
- October 22—"Lady Down on Love" goes number 1.
- Chancery Court master in Nashville Rules that Alabama owes International House of Talent $1,798,825.18 for commissions the agency would have earned during the period of the original contract.

1984

- January—The album *Roll On* is released.
- January 5—The single "Roll On" is released.
- January 24—Alabama debuts four songs from its *Roll On* album on the HBO/Cinemax program, "Album Flash."
- February 28—Alabama wins its second Grammy, this one for Best Country Performance by a Duo or Group.
- March 24—"Roll On" goes number 1.
- April 2—The album *Roll On* is certified platinum.
- April 6—"When We Make Love" released.
- May 14—Alabama wins Academy of Country Music awards as Entertainer and Vocal Group of the Year and for Album of the Year (for *The Closer You Get*).
- June 9—Alabama holds its third June Jam.
- June 23—"When We Make Love" goes number 1.
- July 20—"If You're Gonna Play in Texas (You Gotta Have a Fiddle in the Band)" released.
- September—At the insistence of Alabama and its manager, Dale Morris, RCA withdraws from circulation the "There's a Fire in the Night" video because it does not conform to Alabama's image. The original video has a scene of partial nudity, as well as a bizarre story line. A revised video on the song is reshot in October.
- October 8—Alabama sets a record by being the first act ever to win the Country Music Association's Entertainer of the Year award three years in a row.
- October 26—The single "There's a Fire in the Night" released.
- October 27—"If You're Gonna Play in Texas (You Gotta Have a Fiddle in the Band)" goes number 1.

DISCOGRAPHY

Singles

LABEL & NO.	TITLE	RELEASE DATE
GRT RECORDS		
GRT 129	I Wanna Be with You Tonight/Lovin' You Is Killin' Me	June 23, 1977
MDJ RECORDS		
MDJ 7906	I Wanna Come Over/Get It While It's Hot	circa September 1979
MDJ 1002	My Home's in Alabama/Why Lady Why	January 1980
RCA RECORDS		
PB-12008	My Home's in Alabama/I Wanna Come Over	May 16, 1980
PB-12018	Tennessee River/Can't Forget About You	May 16, 1980
PB-12091	Why Lady Why/I Wanna Come Over	August 29, 1980
PB-12169	Old Flame/I'm Stoned	January 23, 1981
PB-12236	Feels So Right/See the Embers, Feel the Flame	May 1, 1981
PB-12288	Love in the First Degree/Ride the Train	October 2, 1981
PB-13019	Mountain Music/Never Be One	February 19, 1982
PB-13210	Take Me Down/Lovin' You Is Killin' Me	May 7, 1982
PB-13294	Close Enough to Perfect/Fantasy	August 20, 1982

LABEL & NO.	TITLE	RELEASE DATE
RCA RECORDS		
PB-13358	Christmas in Dixie/Christmas Is Just a Song for Us This Year (sung by Louise Mandrell and R. C. Bannon)	November 5, 1982
PB-13446	Dixieland Delight/Very Special Love	January 28, 1983
PB-13524	The Closer You Get/You Turn Me On	April 29, 1983
PB-13590	Lady Down on Love/Lovin' Man	August 5, 1983
PB-13664	Christmas in Dixie/Never Be One	November 4, 1983
PB-13716	Roll On (Eighteen Wheeler)/Food on the Table	January 6, 1984
PB-13763	When We Make Love/Carolina Mountain Dewe	April 6, 1984
PB-13840	I'm Not That Way Anymore/If You're Gonna Play in Texas (You Gotta Have a Fiddle in the Band)	July 20, 1984
PB-13926	(There's a Fire) In the Night/Rock on the Bayou*	October 26, 1984

*From the soundtrack of the movie "River Rat"

 Albums

RCA RECORDS		
AHLI-3644	My Home's in Alabama	May 1980
AHLI-3930	Feels So Right	February 1981
AHLI-4229	Mountain Music	February 1982
AHLI-4663	The Closer You Get	February 1983
AHLI-4939	Roll On	January 1984
AHLI-5339	40 Hour Week	December 1984

AWARDS

1985—Music City News—Top Country Hits Award—"If You're Gonna Play in Texas . . ."
1985—American Music Award—Group of the Year (Country)
1984—Academy of Country Music Awards—Entertainer of the Year
1984—American Music Awards—Group of the Year (Country)
1984—American Music Awards—Country LP of the Year—"The Closer You Get"
1984—American Music Awards—Favorite Video (Country) "Dixieland Delight"
1984—Grammy—"The Closer You Get"
1983—Cash Box—Programmer's Choice Awards—Group of the Year (Selected by D.J.'s)
1983—Cash Box—Programmer's Choice Awards—Album of the Year (Selected by D.J.'s)
1983—Cash Box—Single of the Year
1983—Cash Box—Group of the Year
1983—Cash Box—Vocal Group of the Year—Single
1983—Cash Box—Vocal Group of the Year—Album
1983—US Magazine Award—Favorite Country Group
1983—American Music Award—Favorite Country Group
1983—Grammy—"Mountain Music"
1983—Birmingham Arts Council—Obelisk Humanitarian Award
1983—Music City News—Band of the Year
1983—Music City News—Vocal Group of the Year
1983—Academy of Country Music—Vocal Group of the Year
1983—Academy of Country Music—Entertainer of the Year
1983—Country Music Association—Vocal Group of the Year
1983—Country Music Association—Album of the Year—"The Closer You Get"
1983—Country Music Association—Entertainer of the Year
1983—Billboard—Top LP Artist

1983—Billboard—Top LP Group
1983—Billboard—Top LP "Mountain Music"
1983—Billboard—Overall Top Artist
1983—Billboard—Overall Top Group
1982—Cash Box—Male Entertainer of the Year
1982—Cash Box—Top Group of the Year—Albums
1982—Cash Box—Top Group of the Year—Singles
1982-1983—Alabama Broadcaster's Association "Citizens of the Year "
1982—International Country Group/Entertainers of the Year—United Kingdom
1982—US Magazine Award—Favorite Country Group
1982—Music City News—LP of the Year
1982—Music City News—Band of the Year
1982—Amusement & Music Operators of America—Most Popular Artists of the Year
1982—Billboard—Breakthrough Award—Country to Pop
1982—Top LP "Feels So Right"
1982—Top Singles Group
1982—Billboard—Top Album Artists
1982—Billboard—Top Group of the Year—LP's and Singles
1982—Billboard—Top Artists of the Year—LP's and Singles
1982—Academy of Country Music—Vocal Group of the Year
1982—Academy of Country Music—Entertainer of the Year
1982—Academy of Country Music—LP of the Year—"Feels So Right"
1982—Country Music Association—Instrumental Group of the Year

1982—Country Music Association—Vocal Group of the Year
1982—Country Music Association—Entertainer of the Year
1981—Cash Box—Top Group of the Year—Singles
1981—Cash Box—Top New Group of the Year—Albums
1981—Cash Box—Top Group—Singles
1981—Billboard—New Group of the Year (Selected by D.J.'s)
1981—Academy of Country Music—Vocal Group of the Year
1981—Country Music Association—Instrumental Group of the Year
1981—Country Music Association—Vocal Group of the Year
1981—International Country Group/Entertainers of the Year—United Kingdom
1980—Cash Box—New Vocal Group of the Year—Singles
1980—Cash Box—New Vocal Group of the Year—Albums

(Source: RCA Records)

INDEX

A

B

C

D

E

F

G

H

INDEX

INDEX